The Awakening Manifesto: The Protocols of those who have realized the Truth for a new world

The Awakened Ones

© 2023 The awakened ones

All rights reserved.

Copyright Warning:

This work is protected by copyright law. The author wishes to clarify that no financial benefit is derived from the distribution or use of this material. All compensation, donations, or proceeds generated by this work are designated for charitable purposes.

Any financial support received is intended solely to contribute to charitable causes, and the author and contributors do not receive any financial gain from the dissemination or use of this content.

Conditions for using this work:

1. Attribution: You must clearly acknowledge the original authorship of this work by citing the source and providing a link to the original work if applicable.

2. Non-Commercial Use: You are permitted to copy, share, or adapt this content for non-commercial purposes only. Any use for commercial or financial gain is strictly prohibited, as all proceeds are committed to charity.

3. No Derivative Works: You may reproduce this work in its entirety without modification. Any adaptations or derivative works should be created with proper attribution and follow the same non-commercial and charitable guidelines.

4. No Distribution of Unauthorized Copies: You are not allowed to distribute unauthorized copies of this work that do not adhere to these conditions. Unauthorized distribution may be subject to legal action.

Please respect the terms of this copyright notice, and any support or compensation provided should be directed toward charitable endeavors. If you have any questions or require additional information regarding the charitable contributions, please contact the author or copyright holder.

PREFACE

The following is not the precipitation of baseless delusion nor the manifestation of irrationality. These may seem to be the appearance of such ideas from the outsider, from the point of view of those who indulge in that which they so much criticize. This book, rather, is directed at those who, having attained such aforementioned qualities in positive order, have awakened their true calling and have realized that not all which they have been told can be denominated as truthful. There are countless ways in which people can differ from each other, but the most decisive is that of belief, of thought, of ideals. Human beings are mental beings, "with our thoughts we make the world", with souls we are led either into piercing darkness or into divine glory. The problem is that this belief has been degenerating since ancient times, leading ultimately, unto these days of darkness, to a society of zombies, literally the walking dead; people who think they think, who think they know, who think they love, but of which these is but a front for the inoculation of their evil counterparts. This slumber is happening in the interest of a few, who consider themselves above all of humanity, who consider they have the right to exercise strict control over our lives, over our nature, and ultimately; over our souls. They are truly scared beyond comprehension, and every second, of which they permanently seem to hold acquaintance of, as they themselves claim to never sleep, to hide the truth and plans and abilities which may be created by a group of people to usurp their power, to; above all, awaken the inner spirit of realization within each human being. If there is any wake-up call, they ultimately repudiate the spiritual one, the moral one and rational one. For all these things seem to be contrary to their agenda, and once again, their beliefs, which are, of a Luciferian character, in which licentiousness is above all else, and the basis of life itself is the constant seeking of happiness beyond the mentioned qualities endowed, through logic, to the comportment of every human. Ultimately, this is a battle of good and evil, of ignorance or knowledge, of unconsciousness or wisdom, of light and darkness. This light, which represents knowledge, is not the one offered by this entity by which they so much worship, for this entity is not a manifestation of nature; of perfection, but of rebellion against the same, for it is not a manifestation of universality and infinity, but of limitation of consciousness and morality, and because it is not a manifestation of reason, but distortion and meager casuistry procedures over the disruption of the same in the invocation of their actionality. The only path worth following is that of truth, and they do not stand on that side the universal dual confrontation, but we, as those who have awakened to this ever-going battle between good and evil, between truth and falsehood, light and darkness, are the ones who shall commence the divine labor for the assimilation of these beyond the obfuscations of their counterparts. Which are far more numerous only in the lack of knowledge, but which would soon disappear if this knowledge is ever utilized, in plain aggrupation of misconceptions and division, for the upliftment of the only thing worth in life, truth, wisdom and God, which is embedded within each of us, and which is and has the power to affront any of the negative aberrations who seek to confront his never-stopping tragic-comedy. Therefore, the only truth knowledge, is the one we possess, and the only darkness, ignorance; is the one by which we onlive hell, but not anymore, for this ignorance of the masses, and evil of the few, will be vanquished by light of knowledge and wisdom; or superb benevolence beyond any hypocrisy or conditioning, which, with its omni-directional radiance will illuminate and awaken the truth in the minds of those which, by their slumber, allow those few to dissect our existance, and which by the power of Our Mother and Father, will become the victims of that in which they so much indulge, until the cycles of time so desire it, to resume the presumed and assumed sliding through the paradise of aberration. One which ends as soon as the majority, still in illusionary fervor, renew their energy towards the truth worth indenting obsession. See thus, that the following stanzas are not for the conviction of anyone, except those who are already in such state, to those who have overcome all fear of mis-congruence beyond the commonality of present societal nature, who desire a change, and who are aware of this so-called conspiracy, and its ever manifesting consternations. This book is for all those who have awakened, at least to a low degree, to truths beyond the layers of social masquerades; theaters of darkness, and who know those truths of occult origin which are not to be told in public except in the advantage of welcoming understanding and open mindedness. This book is for you, no matter who you are, to what organization you belong, to what race you were born, or what corporation you are held, if you believe in something beyond, even its bare minimum, beyond the sepulture of officiality, you are welcomed to read the universal plan of us, to widen the spectrum of our awakeness, and to defeat the evil of those who had led us and the rest of humanity, to our previous state. This is the *modus operandi* of the light bringers of society, who, now, are needed more than ever, and which are the, under evident possibility and probability, the only candle to see hope in such a *kali*-permeated society.

1. Knowledge is power

"Knowledge is light, ignorance is darkness | Awakening society to greater truths | Utilizing knowledge for spiritual empowerment | Knowledge as the foundation of battles and deception | Transmission across diverse channels | Spreading truth without jeopardizing our existence | Strategic control of mediums: libraries, online platforms, education | Covert presentation of truth for societal assimilation | Third-party utilization with inner agent control | Targeting conspiracy theorists and spiritualists | Public and covert influence for mutual benefits | Light bringers for enhanced understanding and initiation into our society."

Knowledge is power, knowledge is light, knowledge is that which is required to accomplish anything in life, knowledge is what feeds our curiosity and what adds true resources to our society. Ignorance, on the other hand, is darkness, is all that leads to corruption of mind and further decay of the human mind. The definitive difference between most people is that of knowledge or ignorance. Knowledge, nowadays, is available to all, so it is not only a question of knowledge, for if so it was, every one would be awakened, as information is already available to all if one is to investigate. The question therefore is also of consciousness and wisdom, for if people had any desire to truly free themselves from the yoke of those people, they would rationalize this knowledge of truth no matter how atypical or out of social norm and officiality it may be. The truth is in front of their eyes, and such truth can only be explained by such facts and concepts, yet they continue to deny them. Knowledge, thus, is only valuable if acquired through experience and awakening and if properly conjugated with reason and intuition. If as Sun Zu said, all war is based on deception, and all of such art of deception is based primarily on knowledge, its transference and state within the human mind, we can see that all battle ultimately is one of knowledge, is one of wisdom, consciousness and mind. Whenever knowledge is suppressed, whenever knowledge is directed and grouped in a single point, it is prohibited from the people, and therefore it leads to abuse of power by those who possess such knowledge over those who do not. Therefore, we shall, under all circumstances and through all means, accumulate such knowledge and democratize it for the free utilization of the people, we should provide the people with such knowledge at no cost, we shall take advantage of all physical and digital resources for the collection and exposure of such knowledge to the public. This knowledge will automatically serve as the awakening of more people without further conviction and inculcation of truth through reason. Whenever possible, we should expose such knowledge under another identity other than our own, we should utilize third person and front groups everywhere who impersonate such academic and scholastic purposes of common society, but which, underground, promote everyone's teachings without anyone knowing they are the ones that do so. We shall take advantage of everyone who may be known as a form of dissidence and convince them through whatever methods and agents to publish such information and to speak of them with all conviction. Of the aforementioned resources we shall gather library centers, schools, book shops, and any other kind of center where there is a transmission of information. Many times, we may transmit such knowledge under the pretense of transmitting the officialistic views, but in reality presenting hidden clues to the truth, so it stays in the subconscious mind of the people. The digital counterpart shall also be utilized or whatever other medium may be presented for such transmission. We shall utilize our agents, inside our society or outside of the same, to create such websites, platforms and accounts on all kinds of social media where such information is expressed. We shall take especial care of those groups which are rather in correspondence with the intellectual kind of people, of which we shall entice to the truth by clear proof of the facts which prevent them from following the official dogmatic and criminal ideologies. We shall utilize all of such mediums and processes by which printing and manufacture of knowledge is processed. Our agents shall impersonate being authors on whatever platform it may be and posing as writers, while divaging from one ideology to the other, so no one, the people who shall learn the truths by own enterprises nor our enemies, realize we are the one behind such exposure of truth. Whenever possible we shall not only control or processes of printing, but we shall also control media of all kinds for such ends, including the radio, the TV or any other, in which we shall use our agents, and of which our enemies will not under any circumstances know they take part in our society, for they will everywhere go as spies, and tell the truth of our enemies and the spiritual nature of people, but to never tell neither of these we are the ones behind such missions of their. These media agents shall empathize and relate themselves in their attitudes and manners to all strata of society, and even to appear as promulgating the ideology of our enemies, while subliminally partaking in the overtness of the truth through subconscious, undercover means, which shall as much as possible be seem as rational victimization and identification will their in culture in the eyes of the people. Ultimately we shall utilize these influencers in all platforms, physical or digital, to expose our truth, and even to go as for to expose it through such agents in such seemingly unrelated topics, for example, we could utilize comedy or satire to present the truth undercover and while so doing, never letting anyone know we do, and justifying ourselves under these pretexts which go beyond the limitations imposed by their dictator of the politically correct. We ought to mask the presentation of the truth under the most humble and completely unrelated scenarios, so in no way our true intentions are known to our enemies, but to the people in slumber to which we need to convey the truth. Whenever possible, these agents shall naturally and under no true pretense of such an attitude present the information as their opinions, as their true and utmost feeling. In such a way, such expression of the truth shall be masked as freedom of expression, which cannot possibly be annihilated by the dictatorship. We shall go as far as hiring such agents and placing them in public scenarios and centers such as restaurants, malls, etc, where they shall speak to the people as any other such workers would do, and would to ultimately gain their trust and present their opinions without letting these know we are the ones behind such seemingly natural and common exchange of social order. One may not seem enough, but when we gather many of such agents under all such circumstances, they will add up to numbers which allow as to expand this knowledge and truth under all kinds of pretenses, scenarios and justifications, so let now one know we are behind, to let no one know the true extent of our power, the truth presented to them, its origin, and to find a justification to pass over the mortifications of the dictatorship of officialism. These agents shall be trained to project and inject such truths in a way that best feeds the intellect and opinions of the person to be awakened. They shall present such truths this or that much and to this and to that person, and in this or that way, aligning all these for the proper inculcation of such knowledge in the minds of people. Whenever possible such truths shall be disguised under that which the zombies are most attracted to, as to more easily present and rationalize in accordancc with their own overall personality. We shall present the knowledge, not only in public through covertness, but in secret through overtness, therefore, whenever possible to transmit such knowledge one-in-one in private instances, we shall be permitted to do it with greater fervor, but still never to let such persons know we are the ones behind such agents, later, if the person fully realizes the truth, and awakens once and for all the truth and the slumber society is in, even if the person does not fully present spiritual nature nor ultimate conception and perception beyond the officiality, we shall present the ideas of joining us, but to first join the so called which we shall manage through another agent, which shall be the manager of such institutions and organizations for the transmission of knowledge. These managers of agents shall be the middleman between those which present themselves as outsiders and our insiders, and whenever possible, it shall be discussed when such persons are valuable and advanced enough in their attitudes and aptitudes to join our society, while they are maintained in that front group we manage through the same. These agents which transmit information shall be as light bringers, which bring the truth to the people through all means and circumstances, and who go as far as risking their own lives to let the truth be known out there, while letting no one knows where it is derived, the messengers nor the message, but to present to the people in all naturality and illusion. Because the slept are immersed in the illusion of maya, the truth can only be presented to them through this illusion, whenever we see they are about to escape such illusions, we may pull them to our front light bringing groups, and whenever they have completely escaped maya, and are full of hunger for the truth and spiritual advancement of the whole society, we may pull them to our own center society. When in our society, they shall let everyone know of the truth freely, but never let anyone no one know they are part of our society and to let no one know, hence, it is derived from us.

As these people awaken more and more, let the knowledge presented to them be more and more practical and hermetic, and let them further and further know of our knowledge of the truth and the way by which we communicate, but never let them let others know, especially our enemies in the dictatorship of these. We should especially let this knowledge be known through our agents to politicians and persons which hold any kind of position of influence over the society, may it be political, economical or any other, for they serve as medium by which we can readily promote the truth ingrained in our teachings. Our agents shall always work for us for minimum compensation and they shall do as we order them to do, without any desire for fame, money, women, nor ego, but only for the consummation of this new state of mind we look forward to developing in the greater masses of society. Let them always be humble and remember that they do this solely by their own, by their own convictions of the truths, and by their desires, which accommodate to that of us. We shall also utilize digital medias, platforms and groups to create these light bringing groups in which such information is presented, these shall be further utilized readily and more automatic and resourceful ways, these shall become our specialty, for herein we can express the truth we greater conviction to the young, and well in some cases, to the old, but more especially to the young which can easily be denoted and realized of the truth through our ideology. We shall especially support these youngsters in whatever doubts and misunderstandings they have, for in such cases we further hope from their answer and flexibility to our ideas, and faith to our oath of secrecy.

The knowledge presented by our deeds on this planet, shall, for the most part be of two kinds: spiritual and conspiratory. Spiritual is all that knowledge related to the spiritual practices which we practiced in practicality, and which will outwardly be presented as the means and purposes of our center apparent organization, as well as other kinds of philanthropic and educational knowledge, which we shall present with especially care in each country and in accordance with the ideology of the people therein and the extent to which such laws regarding this knowledge are imposed. But never let any of these 3 kinds of knowledge or light be presented beyond the regulations of society nor of the people in the dictatorship. The conspiracy knowledge, is the truth pure as it is, raw light which is many times hard to swallow, this knowledge is the one which we shall present to the people through our front light-bringing groups, which can refer to the spiritual too, whenever they deem so correct. Through these means, we transmit this knowledge to the main types of people in the awakening process, those interested in spirituality and those interested in conspiracy. Those interested in conspiracy seem to be a wider amalgam of people, for they are particularly influenced by false dissidence and other kinds of extremist ideas and ideologies, we shall always utilize these to promote the raw truth undercover. On the other hand, spiritualists seem to be more inclined to our spiritual practices yet they are still subdued and present in their attitudes with a certain submissiveness to the dictatorship and her demands. We shall utilize these to present the apparent not-out-line teachings and knowledge we possess. It is easier for a spiritualist to be a conspiracy guy, then viceversa. Therefore, we shall always try to turn these spiritualist to the raw truth found in these so called conspiracies, before ever trying to make, many, or quite many of the conspiracy guys spiritual, for, even though they have awakened to some truths, they still are very crude in their perceptions and actions to become an active participant of our extenuating spiritual practices. Let, in definitive, our center society be massed by us solely, those who are engaged in both spirituality and conspiracy. Let us, then, have overt contact with our spiritual alumni of our public organization for the teaching of these truths, let us have overt interest in directing knowledge of donations, charity and educational purposes, always directed through the common regulations of such society in which they are presented, if any of these present such interest in conspiracy, we shall let the agents display them such of these truths so as to further open their eyes. Covertly, secretly, let us utilize these dissidents and many other agents of ours, who we may hire to act as third parties, and who shall promise full allegiance to our cause. They shall be all things to all men, and present this conspiracy raw truth wherever they go, as if they were missionaries of light. They should especially display themselves among groups of such people who like such topics, and always to act as one of them, and to further investigate who among them is fit to become spiritual, given the certainty of their conspiracy knowledge. Whenever any of these alumni, spiritual or conspiracy, is feed, given the conjunction of both of these realizations in their minds, and the advancement of their aptitudes, we shall henceforth let them join our center inner organization, in which we shall present to them our teachings, first through our method of initiation of symbols and allegories, and later through our plain teachings and objects, which may or may not be presented to this person along the way in our inner society. Ultimately there are certain key points in this main protocol of knowledge, regarding especially, the battle between light and darkness, and the battles between these two forces of knowledge and ignorance:

- We know that only thing we know is we know something, yet we know that we hold some more knowledge greater than many in society, and hence, it is our mission to awaken them to such truths.
- We know of the quotes by Sr. Bacon, that "Scientia est potentia", and as such knowledge is to always be utilized to bring the power, especially the spiritual and sagacious one, back to the people.
- We also know because of the aforementioned principle, knowledge is not only power but the foundation of the art of deception and hence the foundation of any battle at all, such as the one we persecute.
- We know that the transmission of such knowledge must in no way be limited to one sphere, but that it must accustom to all channels and recipients.
- We know that our object is to spread the truth and such knowledge, and empower the greater number of people in the shorter period of time possible, but to do so without it dangering our existence through the breach of such actions to our enemies.
- We shall, privately, secretly and publicly control as needed each of the mediums by which such knowledge is to be transmitted, such as: libraries, bookshops, online platforms, media, educational institutions,etc, and in which we shall from time to time use front groups to exculpate ourselves.
- That, contrary to what our enemies do, of lying outwardly, we shall present the truth covertly, and give all denotation and demarcation feasible, as to make it expand all throughout society, even to the extent of unconscious assimilation of the same by the people, such as through and other means of naturality.
- That, to accomplish what has been described in the previous point, we shall utilize whenever possible third parties and that such third parties shall be controlled by our inner agents, which will control these groups and organization and dictate further knowledge of our enterprises to these people, all without letting no one know except our parties of interest/involved.
- That such truth, we shall mainly present to 2 groups of people in society, which are very related to each other, that of conspiracy theorists and that of spiritualist, and that to one we shall present our connection publicly, while with the other covertly, and that we shall direct such groups in our benefits.
- That whenever we deem suitable we shall utilize our trainers and managers, who we shall call light bringers, to improve the understanding and further awakening of these people, and that, when a certain level of knowledge in so-called conspiracies and spirituality has been gained, they shall be carefully induced into our society, later gaining initiation and maintain the promises.

2. The transmutation of evil

"From primitive desires to benevolence | Agents in marginalized and criminal spheres drive positive change | Online vigilance counters malevolence | Guiding rationality and kindness | Addressing addictions through subtle interventions | Embracing Hapkido philosophy for renewal | Adaptive strategies render malevolent energy meaningless | Transmuting ignorance covertly and overtly | Charity promotes goodness."

As powerful as knowledge is the power by which our society is to transmute the inconveniences and evils begotten by its counterpart, ignorance. This evil, which is manifested many times as the personification of the most primitive and animalistic desires of men, shall be transmuted to benevolence and spirituality. We shall, whenever such an incident occurs, and it is in our knowledge, try, through one way or the other, to turn that person to the side of benevolence and spirituality. We should especially take care of sending agents qualified for such purposes in ghettos or marginalized societies where people are given little attention, and where there is a need for guidance. Wherever and whenever there is a need for guidance and evil has taken the upper-hand in the attitudes of a person, we shall guide them with our knowledge and give them opportunity to take part in these third party groups of ours which are to have the object of bringing those people out of those evil enterprises and deeds. We can do this secretly or overtly, but always taking special care and attention in the fact that we shall not let our enemies know we are using these as cards against their possible attacks, but we always do it for the betterment of society and the people to be helped themselves. For such a reason, we can overtly operate with such people by giving them shelters in our care centers and providing them with whatever they need within the normal social norms. Now, when the people to be helped are more prone to criminality and illegal acts, we shall always help them through third parties and our agents of such kind everywhere, agents which shall become themselves as evil as their or purport they so do, all with the purpose of helping these people from within. Whenever any of our members or our society is facing backlashes as results of this evil, we shall transmute it into benevolence, by utilizing our spiritual powers, white magic, and by making this person or people realize that what they are committing is wrong. We shall always, for such purposes utilize third party agents, as this our not of our society according to the apparent knowledge of the evil people we are to change, but who cannot confront the prejudice many times faced by the people enacting such evil deeds. Whenever possible we shall utilize psychologists or through these third parties send these people to psychologists whenever our deeds to transmute their evil are not sufficient, but never let the people to change nor the psychologists know that we are the ones behind the arrangement of such meetings. On the internet, whenever we find evil comments we shall destroy them one way or the other, especially abusive, aberrant comments of degenerate persons such pedophiles in practice or any other kind of such evils, or any other kind of such addictions, by which we should through our agents contact this person, and recommend them the best help possible. Whenever a person has evil or degenerate thoughts we shall try to be amicable to such person, through forums, mediums and centers of community and religion, be they physical or digital, and we shall always change their words and deeds to the positive side of the eternal swing of dualistic energies. Whenever people are taking part in a discussion or confrontation, we shall try to reconcile the peace by dint of beautiful words and points in common, taking always into account, the personality of such people. Whenever we may feel people have bad thoughts or intentions, we shall always address or prevent its consequent externalization by changing the mentality of the person or directing their attention at any other subject while their anger and evil and degenerated thoughts leave their minds. We shall, given this previous example, address all of such evil from their psycho-causal points, just as we address them in our political institutions given the criminality of the people. We shall take especial care of the vibrations ingested and digested by such people through their body, mind and spirit, and to always prevent from further consuming such evil vibrations. For one imbalance in one of the three strata of human expressions can lead unto the other. We shall take care of such evil through a holistic point of view, and change all negative into positive. Evil is also influenced by other negative emotions, and evil is simply a state of vibration in their minds, which has been found to be a combination of negative emotions, and of which we shall change these negative emotions, thoughts and beliefs into positive ones, in that order. We shall first change their emotionality, for this is the utmost expression of human beings, which are very emotional but not rational. We shall take them to rationality and convert their emotions of evil to those of benevolence and kindness. Then we shall proceed to change their thoughts by changing their attention to our words, images or any other instrument we may make use of, finally we shall after some time of conversation, if such is attained, change their beliefs and inner-cause which originate such evil deeds. We shall convince them that such evil deeds are a complete waste of time and that they will not go very far that way, that it would be better for them to be moral, and that every bad actions will return one way or another, one time or the other, open their minds to our ideas of karma and reincarnation and change their feelings from those evil to those of spirit, especially make them aware of the insignificance of such acts and the temporality of their existence, which we shall always utilize to convince them to the good of path of morality, naturality and spirituality, and that this is preferable and apt to give them eternal liberation and salvation from such samskaras they themselves manifest and which do not provide them eternal happiness, but simply ephemeral pleasure. In this sense, evil is like an addiction of which the subject cannot escape, given he has become a victim to his instincts and illogical/immoral ideology. We shall always try to get such people out of such addiction through our third party medium and front groups which shall utilize to get people of addictions such as those of drugs, sex, pornograpy, alcohol, or even coffee or any other samskaras, as apparently meaningless it may be, through this we make sure such subject will become more rect and will be guided towards the path of goodness. We shall always transmit our benevolence through our mediums of expression we have. We shall entice and create ideologies, underground, that will lead people to the path of morality and dharma, in contrast to the prevalent one of evil, and make people aware of the many ways in which they may incur in these, without them knowing of such faults of morality, and without even knowing we are the ones behind such refreshment of memory and fault. We should especially take as reference the Art of Hapkido of the Korean martial artists, which are skilled in the utilization of the force exerted by the enemies to kill the enemy itself, to defend ourselves, and to change whatever evil or attack aimed at destruction for one aimed at renewal and new beginning towards a path of morality. Hapkido denotes by its original etymology the balancing or energy "the way to harmony". Such a way is the same we shall utilize to balance and transmute the energy of our enemies and their evil forces. The similarity is so high that we shall go as far as practicing and emulating this art of Hapkido, we shall learn this martial art and learn from them, and from of these oriental philosophies of such arts the transmutation of the forces of our enemies or that of the people denoting evil we are to change. We shall also provide charity through whatever means and agents we may have to all those who are found in the same cause of us of giving more to the good and transmuting evil people into good people, we shall also promote such acts of transmutation in our educational and religious centers, for in such a way, we further promote these transmutation around our inner-circles and not just for the greater masses. We shall not only transmute evil of others, but we shall always do the same ourselves, and take especial care to use this as a "to all our objects". Whenever any evil is presented between us and our objects, we shall transmute the evil energy exerted by the invokers of such means towards our ends, without realizing that by operating under such evil means and intentions they are benefitting us. For example, if we find an enemy of our wants to destroy our interest in helping or supporting that group of marginalized people, by doing all sorts of rituals of magic or any other kind, we shall rapidly change our deposition and render such acts meaningless or we shall, instead of placing these goods people as our object of support, place evil, especially if such evil people are the enemies themselves, by such rapid changes and flexibility we can render and transmutate such evil energy for the destruction of our own enemies themselves and for the further consecration our ends. The same method shall be utilized for the common people, of which we shall always turn to the good side, that of knowledge, and, in this case benevolence, so that they work towards our ends without them knowing. In such a way, we will gather their efforts and utmost desires to our ends, rendering the means and resources needed for the accomplishment of our ends at a rate of 20% for 80% ends. In such a way, and through such transmutations, of not only evil, but of any other kind of negative thought, belief or emotion which lead to the same, we transmute all negative into positive and all evil into benevolence, all degeneration into rectitude, all war into peace, all irrationality into reason, all materialism and spiritualism, and so on with regards to any other kind of duality. We ought to be as the alchemists, which transmuted metals into others with the help of magic and other occult means. We shall be just like Paracelsus, who said, "Evil is the perverted goodness' ' but shall focus on making such transmutation above all a mental and spiritual factor, and utilize our psychologist, psycho-therapist and spiritual power for the building of the same. We shall effectuate such transmutations through all other protocols we utilize and all our means and ends shall be directed at this "way of harmony", for in such expression we shall render perfectibility, for whenever and wherever there is no peace and harmony, there is imperfection. Whenever we cannot transmute such evil or the invokers of the same, we shall replace the evil or destruction at which the evil directed, rapidly by that which equally evil or friends of actionality with the invoker, so that we may render possible the unconscious destruction of the enemy by their own means, in which case they would learn, and be left in such grief that they will have to change their opinions and turn to the good side of the story. We shall make the utmost effort to render any of these 3 factors, namely, the transmutation of the invokers of message or the messenger of evil, or the replacement of the point to suffer evil by one of goodness. Whenever, we have no other option, and the situation so denotes it, we will have no option but ourselves destroy the messenger of such evil or the way by which this message is sent, which, at many times, will apparently look immoral from the outside but which in actuality is beneficial and dharmic for all parts. For the killing of a killer denotes the killing of killing. To this we shall later refer. Equally, when speaking of knowledge and ignorance, especially of those groups more akin to us such as spiritualists or conspiracy theorists, we shall tranmuste all ignorance which may be contained within their minds into knowledge, we shal change oblivion into consciousness, or vice versa if it so requires it, and we shall changes unconsciousness for wisdom. As mentioned in the knowledge chapter, we shall render of such things covertly or overtly as the situation best fits the existence of the society and confrontations with our enemies and the people in general. We should choose carefully to make such transmutation in public or overtly, and for public means, to utilize our society as it is, through charities, libraries, educational centers, religious centers, etc. And through covert means, we shall always utilize our agents and those which we may utilize in these front groups of we have spoken. These front groups shall be called transmuting agents or transmuting groups, and they shall be utilized for the same just explained transmutation of us and of others, of negative means towards positive ends.

- Our mission revolves around transmuting societal challenges rooted in ignorance, using a meticulous and comprehensive approach. Recognizing ignorance as a breeding ground for primitive desires, we aim to transform these into benevolence and spirituality. Deploying qualified agents in marginalized communities allows us to address unique challenges and guide individuals toward positive paths.

- To counter criminal tendencies, we utilize covert third-party agents embedded in these environments, acting as conduits for positive change from within. Facing societal repercussions, we employ spiritual powers and white magic, converting negative energy into benevolence. Online, we vigilantly counter malevolent comments, recommending help and steering conversations toward positivity.

- Our psycho-causal approach recognizes the interconnectedness of emotions, thoughts, and beliefs. Starting with altering emotionality, we guide individuals toward rationality, benevolence, and kindness. Subsequent conversations reshape beliefs, emphasizing the insignificance of malevolent acts and the ephemeral nature of their existence.

- In response to the pervasive nature of evil as an addiction, we deploy third-party mediums and front groups subtly, targeting individuals ensnared by various addictions. Charity becomes a vehicle for transmutation, ensuring individuals transition towards rectitude and goodness.

- Embracing the wisdom of Hapkido, we integrate its philosophy into our strategies, learning to redirect adversaries' force for renewal and new beginnings. Our strategic transmutation involves adapting rapidly to adversarial actions, rendering malevolent energy meaningless, or redirecting it toward the destruction of adversaries themselves.

- In addressing knowledge and ignorance within groups, we transmute ignorance into knowledge, shifting between oblivion and consciousness. The transmutation efforts extend into public and covert domains. Publicly, our society operates through visible channels such as charities, libraries, educational centers, and religious institutions. Covertly, we utilize front groups known as transmuting agents, serving as instrumental forces for effecting transmutation discreetly.

3. Dharma and self-defense

Resort to raw destruction for dharma's defense against insurmountable evil. | Self-defense arises when evil resists remediation, necessitating suppression of embodiment or immoral means. | Vaporize malevolent evil through secret agents, technology, and spiritual powers.

| Empower the marginalized to covertly combat hidden malevolence. | Infiltrate evil from within, penetrating secret societies, destroying them covertly. | Guided militia and police become defenders of dharma, exposing and combating evil within their ranks. | In the war against evil, remain calm and resolute, defending dharma.

When evil is of such magnitude, that we cannot control through means of relative morality, yet which fall outside the framework of complete destruction of the bodies of such invokers of evil. We will have no option, but to, through destruction, fight against evil through such direct and raw means. This always comes after an opportunity which has been clearly given for such evil to be remediated is not followed, and when we need to protect dharma and the natural right of society. There comes a point in such circumstances, that from time to time present themselves in society, where and when we shall have no option but to fight *mano a mano* against such evil, without no transmutation, given that these have been presented before as transmutations and transformations of character of the victimizer, but which have been obviated, and hence need to be suppressed right through the destruction of their embodiment in this world or through the complete suppression of the means by which such person commits such immoral acts. Any time we commit such acts of self-defense, we do it merely for the vaporization of the aforementioned abuse, of the most evil among the evil, and which leaves no room for transmutation but through the destruction of their means or the invokers of the same. We may commit such self-defense through of our third-party, if such evil is directed against the people, or may use such third-parties and front-groups to protects us of such evil, or in plain language, to assassinate and through whatever means, end the life, or the means by which such evil is operated. Other times, when we have no other option, we ourselves we have to raise, and in all obvious demarcation, will have to defend ourselves against the evil perpetrated against our embodiment or our society and its installations. This defense may take many forms, and many third-parties may take part, in conjunction with us, in the protection of our entity. We shall entice the greatest of the greatest warriors to achieve such protection and self-defense, which may be conducted secretly, in such a way that even the least awaited or seemingly-unrelated person, is capable of offering such protection whenever necessary. We too shall employ such secret and converted means to whenever possible, defend ourselves in the most sinister ways, and through all means, which shall be camouflaged in all kinds of objects and nature at our disposition. We shall also employ technology and spiritual powers of our own to prevent such immoral acts against our personas and the entity by which we hold our existence, this technology shall be unknown to the attackers and the public so the possibilities of counter-attack are minimized, all that is reflected from the point of view of self-defense. Yet it is similar to the means of attack and prohibition of evil. For this one, especially, and when it furthermore comes to our enemies, which yet, do not close to our contact, but which are part of the greater-outer evil, we shall entice our front-groups and third-parties, no matter how poor, marginalized, poor-trained or unknown to the martial arts the may be, to consummate the termination of such evil, and to do so without known that they do it in our convenience. We shall in our spheres of society, however minimum they may seem, send our agents in search of anyone who may have such desire to destroy such evil, and to provide them with the appropriate means and resources we have our disposal, but which we do not use but our only that which we secretly regale to those who seek to destroy evil. Whenever, and under all investigation of its true and genuine intent, we may find a person who has such desires, and such person possesses courage and truly a good person, we shall provide with the means, and exaltations and promulgations of the their intent through our third-party agents, which shall convince such people to commit such act whenever it is so required. In such a way, and through the most humble of means and genuine intents, which flow underground and accommodate to the ones of the most devastated and marginalized of the people, camouflage our destruction of evil and the agents by which such evil is to be destroyed. Never let the people, therefore, know that we are the originators of such evil, for humility and servitude is our most important aptitudes, and the sphere by which our society is so capable of effectuating what is needed without any boost of ego or recognition to our society, in such manners that all our objects, in this case, the destruction of evil after several intents of transmutation, is consummated. Let, especially, the seemingly most vulnerable in society, take arms and grow in certainty and determination in the destruction of such evil, in such a way, the apparently week in society will be empowered for the completion of our ends and the empower of their own, which further strengthens the spirit of our objects and our ideology. Let especially, the young, the children, the women and the elders be empowered, let them have the resources we have our disposal and stop the abuse they often receive in society, but better way to accomplish such a mission than by benefitting our cause and finally ending the invokers of evil of special demarcation, which, precisely and coincidentally, at many times our the ones behind the abuse and disruptors of the dignity of these so-called weak strata of human society. Let equally the poor be empowered, let all those who suffer racism equally be empowered be secretly en-commanded and supported by us in the termination of such evil, even to the point, of not falling under one race or layers of the poverty, but let such empowered soldiers of us take arms in whatever circumstance they may be found, for racism, marginalization and usurpation of dignity and honor can take many forms beyond the one-sided in social order. In summary, let all marginalized and so-called debile layers of society, yet which are of dharmic composition and at which only fault has been the lack of guidance and ignorance, be empowered through all forces, means, resources, exaltations, for the destruction of evil and all those which abuse them. In the same way, the police, the security personnel and all those who outwardly are seen as having this role which they should have of protecting the people against evil, are nothing but slaves to this same evil, therefore they are not of no use to are cause except they awaken to the same we have, therefore, before proceeding to utilize and combines our forces with these, we are to make them join our society before or after they undertake the deeds of being a policemen. They shall provide us with information pertaining to the easier means by which evil can be annihilated, or themselves act in their just right of *bringing* dharma to society. But, under no circumstances let no policemen take part in our inner-society, our organization itself, but let them always, of cooperating with us, take part in one or diverse of our front-groups, without them knowing they are cooperating and fighting in the direction of our objectives. Let them, as they often do nowadays, be corrupt in no way when they are under our guidance, and in no shape or form ignore the wrongdoings of evil, never let them skip over crimes which are usually converted by their conscious and mal-intentioned oblivion, but let them, under our jurisdiction, be truly dharmic police men, and to never look to the other side when it comes to crime. In this same dharmic notion, let them be, above all empathic, to such an extent that they act in the dint of their survival and their protection of the people, yet that they never do so in such fervor that they unconsciously and aberrantly abuse them. Let them, whenever any of these things happen, cooperate for the termination of such evil and the persecution of those policemen who incur and recur into such immoral acts. In such a way, these policemen are to be truly defenders of dharma and raise above the many faults present today in the so called force of order, which, contrary to our dharmic police, submit themselves to the evil of such degenerates dictators and their illogical legislations without question, and in so doing permit the abuse and in some instances, as it has been historically seen, the mass killing of the people in the hands, minds, and chains of these insane governors. In the same way, the militia, which has in its hands the role of supposedly defending their nation against the attacks of others, do nothing but cooperate with these evil forces and further ultimate their relations with entities of demonic nature and aberrant state found within the secret intricacies of Earthly maze. For this reason, and for the reason that war leads nothing but to destruction and the killing of the innocent, they shall be directed to while so being a militant of such militias, hold total loyalty to our ideology through front-groups, and protect, and provide information on the many ways evil is secretly operating in the military, however way possible, without anyone perceiving this incongruency and without any one, not even their family members nor relative in the armies, know that they so act, and let him know not that he in so acting, is proving us with such sacred information, and such important means as those of the military, for with such means we may protect dharma with even more resources and technology and we may further anticipate the same and its early termination for the relieve of the victims or victims of such well-known experiments of trauma and deep-psyche invoked upon human minds, especially women and children. And in conjunction with what had previously been denoted, let them cooperate with these debile sections of society which they and the people that manage them many times abuse, let them empower them and provide with the means by which evil, that evil that precisely slaves them both, is finally terminated. In such a way, both, the "weak" and the marginalized, and the human-beasts which unconsciously betray them and kill, collaborate, by dint of our guidance and resources, towards the destruction and usurpation of the power of those who enslave them, so in such way they are freed from the chains oppression by the true evil in power and their hidden counterparts, and finally they will both ultimately work together for the consecration of our ends, without any of them even conceiving such idea for second in their minds. The role of the militia therefore, is not that of destroying and abusing women, children and unconsciously go to war to follow the order of the equally unconscious generals, yet always roughly conscious of their degenerate acts and subordinations to higher hierarchies, but to support them and cooperate with us in the termination of such war. For war is always a worthless act, one which denotes the confrontation of the civilians and ultimately the destruction of human moral order and dignity, under the command precisely of those who actually need to be killed. Therefore, there is no war of nationality, race or creed for the awakened, but only the war of good vs evil, one which we command with are agents of such kind everywhere, and which, contrary to the zombie who massacres the innocent just for the order and false obligation of the order and act itself, kills for a reason, for a true purpose, for the defense of dharma, of truth, and benevolence and morality, of the betterment of all humanity, and ultimately, for the attainment of our ends, ends which are universally outlined in the Laws of the All, and hence, are aligned with the ends of the these militants themselves. Therefore, anyone who serves us, wil serve humanity and will serve themselves, and ultimately, will serve God and the All. In deeper stances, if we see, to infiltrate into evil itself, and penetrate their realms from within, we have no way of doing than through our third-parties in the marginalized communities and ghettos which we outwardly and publicly help in our inner-society, first, because they are open, free and easiest for us to collaborate give orders too, for no one will be suspicious in this work in marginalized communities, in which criminalize is hugely part of their lifestyles, that when we help, we actually command them to transmute such desire for evil, anger and revenge, into desire to help humanity, and that, if there is anyone to kill or any degenerate act to commit, it is to help God and kill those evil superiors who abuse us, and instead of them abusing and committing such animalistic acts against their own people or distant family, they shall transmute this animalism from abuse of their kind to the destruction of the supreme evil and their agents everywhere upon this world. There is no way to destroy evil, but through evil itself, than through anger, revenge and its true and ultimate transmutation into destruction for the tribute of dharma. In such a way, these agents will prepare the way to our objects of such kind, and in such a way justify such supposedly terrible acts into the defense of dharma and acts which are necessary to follow, because of the anger of the society, for the greater masses of people truly needed this to free themselves from all such abuse. Therefore, this many times prejudiced and marginalized evil which is found within the streets shall be utilized to destroy the evil which is evil to the point of secrecy and remains unperceivable for the same people, the evil itself secretly subdues and keeps in a state of slumber, and which ultimately, leads, due to their evil and greed, to poverty and hence, to the unnecessary creation of evil within such ghettos and marginalized sections of society. Therefore, such marginalized people, which everyone ignores, are gracefully utilized and guided by us towards our objects, and they, in their particularity, shall be directed as specimens of example and differentiation within the greater masses. We can produce, with these uncommon elements within social order, soldiers of awakening, which destroy all that which oppresses and suppresses their true persona and their true desires. Who, by their inherent distinctness, help us utilize their distancing from the common submission for the awakening of the masses, and their deeping sleep delusions in which critical thinking and questioning is never present. Through all these means, we can convince these people to follow our path, and to, through all our tentacles of psychological order, persuade to follow our path, and to assure in their determination that there is not other path for the termination of their marginalization and abuse but the greater masses in command of the chiefs of evil but through such means predisposed by us. For whatever reason they are abused and ignored, it is by that same reason that they shall follow our commands, for they will be awakened to the fact that in their attitudes and aptitudes, or those of physical order by which they are marginalized, are the same reasons which have awakened to in our truths of spiritual and conspiratorial order, yet that same marginalization and distinction from the slumbering masses have been ordained under the same fundamental factor: the lack of knowledge, consciousness and wisdom from the people, and therefore to their lack of true morals and benevolence; in such fact, we both agree to this great truth and we can collaborate with these victims of solitude and exculpated degeneration towards that which truly needs to be persecuted and marginalized, the chiefs of true evil on top of the ladder, which through secrecy, destroy and secretly consume the soul purpose of each of us, and that, in first instance, are at fault of the current state of society and hence the mutilation of the quality of life of these marginalized, and the mere existence of people like us in such a distypic and brutally aberrant world, one separated from its divine inner-nature and cosmic connection, one which we shall bring back through these methods previously mentioned, and the awakening of the flame in those which are at most victims of the same, and the dimishing of the concievers of the aformentioned. Eventually, we may have not other option but to let these agents of ours infiltrate in all imitation and naturality into the core of the chiefs of evil themselves, let them infiltrate in their secret societies and destroy them from within, while pretending they do the contrary and the collaborate with them, but never to truly indulge in it, let them be hypocrites in all attitudes and sense, so nor their benevolence is recognized by the evil nor their evil by the benevolence, but remain in all determination in the middle as a multifaceted man, working solely for us in secret, and saying to himself, the only good and evil is that is to be done according to the commands of the awakened people. Let them through such manners, therefore, remain in a state of they can blindly follow our orders in reach a state where there possible "evils", are secret directed at our dharmic objects, and there possible "goods", are only the evil inwardly presented to the secretive elements to be destroyed, so these are "goods" are the real ones, totally inconceivable to the people. But let, in all times, be conceivable to no one but ourselves.

By such previous manners, we shall imitate Krisha and his teachings to Arjuna in the battlefield, and remain, in conjunction with our agents, as calmed and rect in the midst of war as we are the midst of the utmost peace of our spiritual practices, and stand at all times ready to defend dharma at all costs, even if we have to kill our own blood and countrymen, for we, and our society defend dharma, we and our society will be defended by the same. And many times, such defense will take the form of violence, one which we effectuate with the utmost reasons, honor and composure, and that if done, is done in all assurance that it will bring the end to the death of so many more lives taken by the life taken itself. Let us therefore, never in such struggle against the usurpers of dharma upon the faith of the Earth, be led discouraged into fear and irrationality, but to keep these at all times for the salvation of our humanity.

- In the face of insurmountable evil beyond the confines of relative morality, a resort to direct and unfiltered destruction becomes an imperative response. This drastic measure is considered when opportunities for remediation are blatantly disregarded, and the protection of dharma and societal order becomes paramount. Self-defense, in this context, is not merely reactionary but strategically executed after careful evaluation of the failure in transmuting evil through other means.

- Secret agents, equipped with technology and spiritual prowess, are enlisted to empower marginalized segments of society. These covert defenders are instrumental in the clandestine battle against hidden malevolence. Their role extends beyond individual protection to the transformation of the seemingly vulnerable into formidable forces for societal betterment.

- Furthermore, the strategy involves infiltrating the very core of evil structures. Guided militias and police personnel, previously seen as potential obstacles, are transformed into defenders of dharma. By covertly exposing and combating evil, these forces contribute to the subtle unraveling of malevolent agendas.

- The commitment to defending dharma involves not only direct confrontation but also a nuanced approach. Calm resolve in the midst of chaos and the strategic use of unconventional means are emphasized. This includes infiltrating evil from within, utilizing militia and police in a covert manner, and maintaining an unwavering stance against usurpers of dharma.

- In this complex and multifaceted struggle, the narrative draws parallels to the teachings of Krishna to Arjuna in the battlefield. The call to defend dharma at all costs, even if it means confronting one's own kin, underscores the unwavering commitment to a higher cause. The acknowledgment that violence may be an inevitable tool in the defense of dharma is approached with reason, honor, and a composed demeanor, all for the salvation of humanity in the face of prevailing malevolence.

4. Our family is universal

"In our cosmic society, universal love transcends worldly dogmas, seeking cosmic objectives. | Countering the virus of moral relativism: Befriending all races and classes openly or secretly, infiltrating enemy circles, transmuting, and strategically operating. | Primitive societies hold wisdom, aligning with our natural order: Gaining access to less-known lands through unknown tribes. | Universal love extends to animals, ending unnecessary suffering, and utilizing psychic capacities. | Flora and fauna are guided by our practices, covertly utilized for objectives. | Minerals, guided by universal ethereal energy, serve constructive or destructive means. | A special empathic relation with the All includes befriending entities beyond dimensions, strategically utilizing wisdom and resources. | We

embody universal, rational, spiritual, and natural principles: Connecting authentically with the truth and God within the All, balancing love and destruction as needed."

As a follow-up to what has been said in relation with the marginalized people, we extend this process of universalization within our society in this chapter. We, as a society, pertain to a universal family, one which is cosmic and which is so cosmic in relation to our practices gaining a consciousness which expands in the full extent of the universe. Therefore, our consciousness extends beyond the realms and dogmas of limitation within this world. Our love is unconditional and universal, it may take many forms and it may for this very reason of its need of universality, extended covertly under many thoughts, beliefs, emotions and facets, but its key element of unconditionality and seeking of universality always remains therein. Therefore, our love is one which takes many forms, and which extends beyond any meaningless mundanity, so much that it takes advantage of the same to be further extended in time, space and person within a society so opposite to the vibration and delineations of the same. Therefore, we shall entice everyone to be our family, we shall display our love to all, no matter how different, inferior in the intellectual, technological and psychic spheres they may be, for all, as meaningless as it may be, has been expressed upon the all for a purpose, and hence it deserves to be treated with consideration as the life and object of the same found within our own. In such a way of universal loving, we may whenever and wherever it so deems it, utilize this universal family for our own purposes, for with all caring for all, we may extract the means and subterranean paths of all, and we may utilize such universal soldiers for the consummation of our objects. This neo-humanism, which extends humanity beyond humanity itself, permits us and differentiate us from the evil chiefs which control our enemies, and which have some kind of special specism, of such high degree that they are always led astray to the destruction of themselves. Therefore, why shall we fear those that by their illimitable sense of disgust to all, are lead to the bloodshed and killing of their so-called brother and sisters, when we love all, and we feel a sense of attraction towards all? Why are ones victorious and the other "losers" under such distinctions in their family? This is the precisely because the family of this planet is universal in its universality, and we the awakened people, are special in our universality. In such conditions, we are led to camouflage under so many differing ideologies, which, even if opposite to each other, remain true in their conjunction as their distinction from our true sense of unconditional love towards the All. Therefore, this universality of moral relativism survives as a virus which extends itself through ignorance, corruption and animalism, and in some instances, the lack of activity by the true moralism of neo-humanism, which is so common in this era. Thus, we are to find all methods to end this sort of discrimination and lack of morality in conjunction with lack of universality, by ourselves, agglomerating to all those structures, which as narrated before, has been ignored in this society. First, within human society, we are to befriend, openly or secretly, all races, nations and classes of human society. No matter how seemingly primitive or indulgent with our enemies such people may be. First, because in some sense, such primitive people are actually more knowing, consciously or unconsciously, of the laws of naturality within the all, and through these primitive practices our actually more aligned with the logic and spirituality of our order than those so-called civilized people, which are enslaved by the illogical ideologies which have stemmed from such renaissance of our ideals, and which are enslaved to the technology and material and economic mechanisms arising from the same. These primitive societies, such as the indigenous and aboriginal people all over the world, shall be left alone and have free-determination, let us present them our spiritual practices in accordance, as much as possible, with their own traditions, so that they may not feel as being enculturated and conquered by us, but to feel that in such practices they have found the flexibility to keep their traditions and language, which we may at any time so required learn to infiltrate, in the noblest and genuine sense of the word, within their departmentalizations of social order. Let us therefore, not treat them as inferior, as the our enemies do, but let us treat them as our equal, for we deeply know that within their seemingly primitive state there is a liberty, rationality, naturality and spirituality, very much aligned with our own doctrines and rationalizations, from which they could learn and get advantage of, as much as we could befriend for all our means and order, and for the further improvement of our society and the awakening of the social masses. Let us, when presenting to them the so-called civilized world, assure ourselves to teach them how important it is to keep their traditions and liberty held previously and to denounce with total rationality those new unnatural ideologies brought about by the false civilized societics. Let us, whenever so possible, train since their youth to our system, and to let them practice our spiritual and moral doctrines since a young age, so we can quickly make them and train to whenever we may require them, utilize their spiritual powers and consciousness developed in distinctions from the masses in slumber for the benefit of our society. Let all this be done, as much as it has been said before, with full cooperation, kindness and flexibility, for in such a way we distinct ourselves from the other priests, and evangelizers, and for in so doing we make keep their trust and further utilize their means for the benefit of our own order, and evidently, for the benefit of themselves. On the other hand, of those which are said to hugely cooperate with our enemies, we shall at all times infiltrate from their layers of social order, without they knowing that we do so, to as previously mentioned transmute and destroy all evil within those order, and to even go as far as utilize those primitive people mentioned to bring them back to our ideology, from the so-called primitive to those who hold the greatest power within the structure of the matrix. Let us, in such groups of top in which many of our enemies our found, befriend those which our marginalized within their circles, so that we may use their anger and disparity with the majority or greater part contrary to them for our benefit and the corruption and evil found within many of them, whenever and wherever it is so required. In such a way, the evil found within such groups which are distinct in their intelligence and smartness to penetrate and lullaby the society can be destroyed by us, and at the same time, utilized their special qualities for our own means and objects, which at many times, may align with those professed by them. In such a way, we gather many distinct people at the top of the social ladder, and we may further operate through them for a greater proximity with those which possess power to influence and change social order, and which have the aptitudes to awaken the rest of the social masses. Let us equally navigate through the common men and women in between these two extremes as we would do with anyone outside our society, let us be momentarily, and only outwardly in a state of slumber just like them so that we may gain their trust and utilize them for our purposes whenever the circumstance so deserves it. These people may be of any race, nationality, gender or ideology, but they all ought to be equally guided under the lamp of truth without them knowing that they cooperate with us. Let us not act as this common man does with their own common brother and sister, but let us befriend them contrary to their modes, with no utter prejudice and with the correct discernment, so that, no matter how distinct to any member or the majority of the members of our society they may be, especially in terms of race and ideology, they may be guided by our light and contribute to our purposes, let us, especially, befriend a black man with our black men, whites with our whites and yellows with our yellows, let our men, anyhow and any who their characteristics may be, align with those of these great masses, so that they may never be suspicious and open to judge us and condemn us due to their irrationality. Let them, therefore, be guided by us, each and every of these facets of the common men, without even suspecting that in their seemingly equally confronting distinctions they are equally supporting our purposes of destructing evil. Let us therefore, especially among these commoners, take any form in accordance with the illusion within the illusion we want to portray so that they may escape from the same or collaborate with us in the destruction of the same. Let us especially befriend even the most unknown groups of people on Earth, those tribes which are the least in number, those who hold the most extremes and apparently crazy ideas, be entrusted to our guidance, and let them, in their lack of recognition by the people openly operate to our means and ends without even having to do it so secretly, for the people does not even suspect that these groups exist, and hence their existence, and modes of action and their subordination to our order, directly or indirectly, may be unknown to society. By such means of universal control of human society, we may gain access and possession of these less—known lands and we may collaborate with these people easily and without the pressure from the greater masses. Let us befriend, contrary to the common, every and any thing beyond humanity itself, let us be the utmost representation of neo-humanism, for in such love for ALL, we may find the infiltration, transmutation of our for our own means and ends whenever and wherever we may so need it. Let us,whenever possible, end animal suffering, especially when this suffering is utterly unnecessary. Let us further infiltrate farms and other places where such animals are slaughtered and let us finish such unnecessary means whenever it may be possible, let us support animals, for in such a way they may support us. Let us take especial attention to animals which posses especial psychic and spiritual capacities, for they may collaborate with us under the most especial and needful circumstances, and so that no one could, nor the greater masses nor our enemies, conceive that such ends have been arrived at through the surprising and unexpected use of these animals, which they so much abuse in unnecessary means and irrational order. Let us learn the most from these so-called beasts, especially in terms of their natural inheritance and especially nobility and ingenuity. Let us imitate and transmute the characteristics of every animal for our own order, let the best of these qualities found not only in these but anything else, be added up to our order and its mediums, so it may be further efficient, and practical, and perfect in her operations. Let us possess animal trainers, which having qualified these animals to be our soldiers, participate with us, in the most coveted and subterranean ways through the whole of our channels of operation and further render our plans, in such surprising ways, to consummate and do so as a sign of revenge and empowerment for all the harm such an aberrant society has committed against them. Let these animals, according to their arena of expression and deeper participation through their qualities, let the birds operate as messengers and watchers of the areal arenas. Let them be engaged in vigilance without no knowledge of the same of all those who we may be interested in investigating. Let dogs be deeply loyal to our orders, let them especially act in conjunction with our police of dharma and their operations in deeds of blood when it comes to drugs, and other events of criminal order. Let cats, dolphins and elephants, and others of these deeply psychic and spiritual animals be used for our spiritual unfoldment and the same resulting in that of these beasts and their guidance, together with us, to best society. Let them, from time to time, cooperate and participate in these rituals and let us learn what and awaken our perception to their natural reason found within their genuine wisdom. In such and such manner, with each and every animal, we may find the means to utilize them, or rather, cooperate with them in our objects. Let us, as previously stated, differentiate ourselves from our enemies in the treatment of these animals and in the way we reflect the same to the masses, so that there is no doubt we are the standard and the example to follow in the times to come by any decent rational person. Let, not only fauna, but flora be guided and further strengthen by our practices, let us never operate in our ecological cities, operate under the modification, artificial practices of agricultural order nor in the damnation and insulation of the same plants, for in so doing we kill that which we eat before putting it in our mouths. For our spiritual elevations we ought to bless this food and imagine that its vibrations are being those of a positive kind. Let us further, recognize the curative and poisoning qualities of all these plants through our experts in botany and let us use the same, which have been provided by the creator for the rage and revenge of those who break his Laws of Creation. Let us have such natural knowledge of the qualities and properties of all such plants, and let us through this deep knowledge and comprehension of their inner-vibrations guide them covertly and gracefully to the consummation of our objects. Let even minerals, which are to be utterly comprehended and transmuted for the Creation of resources and the manufacturing of our technology, get all our love, and let us, through our engineers of all kinds, utilize this same love and positive vibrations, and within the framework of the the Laws of Creation, accomplish our means, may they be of constructive or destructive order, one always representing the 1% of the order, but always being equally efficient and universal in their conjunction. We shall also not forget that all such elements in their most basic forms, such as in their 5 elemental states, and that all these are all equally guided by the eternal and universal ethereal energy, which is a fragment of Creation itself. Let us hold a special relation of empathic order with the All with All in this world, and even beyond. We may, in such instance, befriend entities beyond this dimension and world, entities which we many time encounter in our spiritual practices and especial reunions, and which if evil, we shall invite to our universal love, and further destroy them and learn how to defend ourselves if it is so needed, other of these extra dimensional and terrestrial entities we may totally and openly befriend, under the prospects of common knowledge and with complete comprehension that their existence is evident, yet many within the social masses completely ignore to the point of mockery, but which precisely us, because of our deep consciousness know the existence of and know that their wisdom and influence in our history is nevertheless present everywhere. Hence, we cannot pass on the knowledge, resources, technology and, above all, wisdom found within such entities of macro-cosmological impact, one which is nevertheless equally strong in this planet and which our enemies secretly befriend in their evil counterparts, but which we equally befriend whenever possible and we combat through with their enemies in the cosmos, which further render us knowledgeable of the evil and benevolent, and therefore with deeper information, resources and means for the usurpation of such relation of the same, through the eons of time, with these enemies of ours. We ought therefore, to be ALL things to ALL, anywhere and everywhere, anyhow and somehow, whenever and always, to anyone and everyone, being, like that ethereal energy and supreme consciousness within Creation that is within All, which first, as us, holds the flag of love and compassion, but, whenever there is any of such imbalance, there is no way but to remediate the same through destruction. After all, we ought to be universally universal, rationally rational, spirituality spiritual and and naturally natural, finding in these redundancies the authenticity and true connection with all which is not truly held with our enemies, for they only look for the benefit of themselves, while we look for the benefit of the truth, and hence, of God, and All within the All.

- "In steadfast adherence to the mandate of dharma, covert operatives engage in strategic endeavors, wherein shadows seamlessly intertwine with a purposeful orchestration of malevolence's demise. The manifestation of destruction converges with tactical sagacity, encapsulating the essence of strategic combat in its covert sense.

- The ethos of universal love emerges as a guiding light, fostering a cosmic kinship wherein consciousness expansively transcends established boundaries. A nuanced empowerment of the marginalized takes precedence, as the societal paradigm undergoes a transformative shift toward a holistic cosmic family, unequivocally visible to all discerning eyes.

- Embarking upon the tenets of neo-humanism, an enlightened fellowship endeavors to establish amicable relations with diverse races, tirelessly navigating the intricacies of camaraderie both in daylight and the shadows. A comprehensive integration extends to encompass the sentient realms, traversing the realms of fauna, flora, and entities residing beyond the known.

- Penetrating the layers of adversaries' lairs becomes a meticulous art form, executed with the finesse of an expert stratagem. Allies are judiciously assembled, and affiliations fostered with sagacious discretion, transcending the tumultuous currents of societal discord. A testament to universal bonds, such affiliations collectively define and illuminate the societal narrative.

- Within the purview of this comprehensive alliance, fauna and flora stand as indispensable collaborators, their inherent qualities transmuted to forge an equipoise between the forces of good and the malevolent. The mineral kingdom, as a strategic resource, is harnessed through expert engineering, seamlessly aligning with the eternal laws of creation.

- Engaging with entities that transcend dimensions, an intellectual communion unfolds. These entities, though enigmatic to the layperson, are dissected, comprehended, and navigated with a scholarly precision that befits the erudition of those advocating universal truths.

- A mandate emerges to be all things to all, epitomizing a universal embrace that transcends the constraints of race and ideology. Truth, as an unwavering lodestar, guides every endeavor, anchoring the collective consciousness authentically in the tapestry of a universal connection that intertwines with the very fabric of existence."

5. The power of the spirit and the Laws Of Creation

Embrace the infinite power within each soul for spiritual enlightenment. | Transcend rationalization and visualize deeper truths for spiritual evolution. | Distinguish yourself through a unique perception beyond conventional understanding. | Explore other realms, dimensions, and realities with enlightened tolerance. | Demystify spirituality through reason, not superstition or dogma. | Master spiritual sciences and counteract dark forces with deep knowledge. | Embrace a universal approach, transcending limitations of specific religions. | Integrate emotional intricacies with scientific exploration for holistic spirituality. | Practice meditation, oration, and visualization for spiritual perfection. | Uphold the Laws of Creation—spirituality, naturality, and morality—as absolute guides. | Initiate spiritual education from a young age, sculpting beacons of enlightenment. | Illuminate truth without fear, gaining trust and support of the masses. | Outshine darkness with our infinite spiritual wisdom, ensuring victory.

Following what has been lastly said in the previous chapter relating to the power and universality of the ethereal element or elements, we shall further add up to such means of spiritual order. There is nothing by which we differentiate more as awakened than our knowledge of the infinite power of the spirit within each and each man and woman. This is so in reference with our Taraka Brahmas and other religious figures we admire for their truthfulness and authenticity in terms of spirituality. Especially the saints of India, Europe and some of them in the Middle East, which are prophets and distinct in such an age of darkness. As Jesus said in some apocryphal scripture, we are to be totally aware of that which is truly valuable, that which is eternal, and therefore of truth, wisdom and absolute validity. Namely; the Infinite power of the spirit and the Laws of Creation. The infinite power of the spirit is simply the powers of all souls given they are a fragment of Creation, or of God's if it is so better understood or adequate to the ideals of the reader. This power is beyond everything else, this power stems in the human mind for the mere fact that the same mind which has GOD, generated, operated and destroyed the universe is able to equally bring about the greatest miracles, manifestations and possibilities, which are infinite and universal in their powers, just as this mind within the All, or this spiritual power within Creation. It is always the thought, which precedes the experience, it is always the spirit which guides the matter and not vice-versa. Hence, the single progress which rules out and manifests with total aptitudes the others is that of spiritual kind, not of physical nor intellectual kind, for ultimately these subordinate to the former are. This same power of mentalism, which is mentioned in many esoteric books is the one by which we are so different, for we further enjoy of a perception which is beyond the common rationalization and visualization of reality, and hence, it is open to other worlds, worlds, realities, understandings and conception which are hand in hand in causal and psychic factors with spiritual evolution and the realization of truth. For this reason, it may be said that such people that have awakened to this truth are inherently more spiritual and more developed in their consciousness than the others, even we shall, from the moment of their conception. We may also say that these people are tolerant in a different way than the masses and open their perception to ideas not common or which stand out of the comfort zone. In this we may also find that the masses live embedded in a single way of rationalization due to their fear, lack of ideals and decay into mediocrity and falsehood within the apparent, something by which we distinct ourselves from this common majority. We may possess an intelligence of spiritual or ulterior order which stands beyond all the other intelligences, an intelligence which is not at all related with the material or the common expressions of human mind, but which are rather directed at a greater sense of idealism, deepen knowledge or mysterious ideas, which to be understood, the mind necessitates to be at a level of tolerance of other realities, dimensions, conceptions and understandings not present in the common fellow. We shall take advantage, as much as our enemies do, of this power of the mind and the spirit, and utilize and reach a level of perception in the same which is equal in its power, yet opposite in its vibrations to that of our enemies and the common people. Let us develop this power through spiritual practices of all kinds, and through all modes of expression, yet is at the core of our ideals there is a common link, a link of love and deeper understanding, a desire to be freed from the illusion in which we are induced, together, unfortunately, with the masses, due to the mechanism of deceit of our enemies. Let this spiritual practices be studied in total logic and rationalized conception, which is the meaning of science, and let us applied and investigate this science of the power of the mind and the spirit, not with superstition or dogmas, but, contrary to the common religions with the utmost reason, yet in the same degree in its level of authenticity and lack of the so-called found within these intuitional and mystic practices and abilities. Let us be the utmost erudite in terms of irrationality, let us apply rationality to this, so that we may find reasons and logic in something which many times is intentionally depicted as illogical or out of balance with the natural law and order. Let us therefore understand the science of spirituality, of the metaphysical, of the invisible, of the astral, of the ulterior, and in short, of all that which may be, for one reason or the other, out of our perception and understanding of reality, or better said, of the common man. We shall find an explanation to these miracles and spiritual events which are said to be superstitious by the common materialist intellectual, let us convince these, and above all, ourselves, that there must be a logical explanation to all such events within the laws of the all and its ethereal connotations, and therefore, let us, in this knowledge of the power and mechanisms of the mental and spiritual develop even greater powers to manifest them, and evoke such miracles whenever we so need them, for none understands these processes better than we do. Let us, as has previously denoted, understand the human mind and psyche as no group has even done so, and let us use the power of our spirit and mind at will in the blink of an eye, so our miracles and power of mystic order may destroy our enemies whenever it so deems it. Let us always, avoid all illogical explanations and dogmas of spirituality and the role of consciousness in the all, but let us always be disgusted by such deceivers which claim to be this or to be that, to do this and to do that, let us be completely secular in our spirituality and spiritual n our secularity, so we may render, and conclude the effects of one world upon the other, and vice versa. Let, all that which we may invoke in the fields of the spirit therefore, be of positive vibration and simple practicality, for nothing is more truthful than the simple, and nothing is more ideal than the practical, always within the deeper meta-commonalities of the slumbering human society. Let us gain such powers by such deep understanding and knowledge of the truth and the expulsion of all dogma and senseless ritualism from our society, let us be distinct in that all we do has a purpose and a reason to be effectuated, and let us always judge our culture as we already have done so, since the moment of our awakening to this state of union and realization, which is to further lead us to one of these states as we progress in our spiritual practices. Of these spiritual practices let us be knowledgeable of them all in rational manners, even of the negative ones, for we shall know our enemies as we know ourselves, so that their destruction may be more easily executed by our agents. Let us have more knowledge of the brains, the psychic and spiritual, and esoteric than our enemies which are expert of such black and dark practices known as black magic (to which we may destroy through our vast spiritual power which extend beyond the 4th dimension by meditation, farther than those reach by this black magic, or which we counteract with its white counterpart whenever so we deem it), let us even develop an understanding deeper than theirs of these practices and the entities which are invoked by the same, so that such extravagant and abundant knowledge we may be victorious, in knowing both ourselves, and our enemies, in the faults and virtues of us both. Let us have wide knowledge especially of the practices and science of spirituality found in India, which seems to be the most scientific and rationalized among all others, let us be experts of the Sanskrit language in the same level as Taraka Brahmas, let us know that spiritual intricacies and etymologies of all language, of all sound and of all symbol, for in so doing we may extract the inherent vibration of such order found within as many of them, as further rendering our enemy's attack useless and without power. No one shall be greater erudites of yoga, its history and practices than us, let us develop an understanding of all their practices and intricacies, so that we may become ap in the most rationalied religion in the world, and hence the most aligned with our ideology of reason within the spiritual and the metaphysical. Let us therefore present ourselves, mainly as a hinduist society but let our understanding be secular in that it will extend beyond the same, contrary to other societies of the same order, which are so dogmatic as to not extend their understanding of spirituality beyond their type of religion in practice. Thanks to this knowledge of Sanskrit and the most scientific among the spiritual practices, in all her varieties, we shall render our abilities victorious over that of our enemies, if such is not the case, let us bring the second card, and execute the same positive vibration of positive and mental order with the occult knowledge of the nature of enemies, and their faults which may render their spiritual powers meaningless. Let our language of deep erudition and understanding as Latin is that of the catholic orders, so that we may find new waves of intellectuality within the meanings and intricacies of such language, which we may further utilize in the future in the materialization of the new ideal society we want to bring about. But let this knowledge and the outlook practiced towards the same be logical and scientific and pragmatic in its understanding, yet let us develop our spiritual and practicalities of the same to the level of that of a maha-yogi. In such a way we do not only only understand the spiritual world, but we practice daily to the liberation of our souls and our union with the All, given the preceding understanding of these spiritual philosophies and her man laws. Let us too, not be encrusted solely in one way of thinking, but let us become as knowledgeable of the mystics and saints of the abrahamic religions, let us above all, love the practical spiritual practiced by such mystics and saints, and as they do, rationally practice what the scribes and Pharisees irrational do not practice, but outwardly use to deceive the people, let us adapt their same saintness and practices even in religions outside the dharmic and abrahamic, so we may find more various way of being victorious over the many practices of the opposite nature. Let us also do not forget, that we shall understand the emotional, concentrational and idealizational intricacies of the spiritual practices and the path by which these flow, for this are very important in the formation of these perfect spirituality, which takes into account all order which relate to its formation, in a holistic and macro-cognizant order, just as it is seen in the scientific perspective. Let us therefore, go even further than the hinduism practices, and understand ALL sorts of scientific relations of emotion, wisdom, allegories, and cycles and mechanisms of the human body and brain with the spiritual practices leading to the liberation of humankind from the cycles of birth and rebirth, for in such a way we may find the path spiritual perfection and progressive yet continuous liberation of humanity. But we are to always, even when possessing such deep understanding, find the path towards perfection through practicality and simplicity, for these together with their unfoldment towards the mental-objectification of our minds towards the eternal, will render us closer to God and the eternal mind than any other group. We ought to be apt in all kinds of spiritual practices and contemplations, such as meditation, oration, and visualization, and to deeply study all the interconnections of the mental in man, and the relation with the spiritual in the All. Let our practice and consummation of our objects not only be permeated by such aptness in the spiritual within all religions of the world, but let us utilize the most common resources and simple of suggestions and hypnotic controls whenever this one is more practical and efficient in the means which lead to the whatever object we may propose. Let us especially render practical the works of suggestion, auto-suggestion, hypnotherapy and many other which may lead the mind to the states we desire, by which we may access realms beyond our own which we may need to voyage, or by which we may easily manifest that which we desire or need our agents or those we help awaken, become more spiritual and support in their difficulties in the material word. Let us, too, possess no greater and vaster knowledge of such sciences and utilize them to help people, in all our charities, support and defend the innocent people, so that we may manifest, in short identification of means, through the infinite power of the spirit, and the same expressed within our deeper layers of the mind, that which we may need from ourselves or from other, for ourselves or for others. With this knowledge of the esoteric we shall render what we desire with the utmost simplicity and naturality, one which as Jesus so used, would be inconceivable to the common man, totally ignorant of the infinite power found within themselves. As the aforementioned had said, we ought to ask, and it shall be given to us, we ought to seek, and we shall find it, we ought to knock the door and the door shall open to us, we ought to believe and so it shall be, we ought to imagine, and so it shall be created, we ought to fight, and we shall be victorious, we ought to discern, and we shall finally separate what is worth and from what is not, and transmit the same knowledge to the masses. We may render any of these qualities of the mind through the most natural, efficient and simplistic means, always with the total consciousness of the infinite power within each of us and the Laws of Creation. For this reason, finally being deinterlaced, we shall refer to the Laws of Creation as the Laws of Nature, as the Laws found within the logics and intricacies of the All. These logics, contrary to the countless and never-ending diffuseness of the men, are absolute and invariable throughout time, and hence they are they true laws of human conduct, contrary to the laws of Men they are few in number but hold, in their truthfulness, a value infinitely superior to that of the relative laws established by men. These, in our rationality, are 3 in number, they are those of spirituality, naturality and morality, we shall be the objectification and personification of these laws according to the best means we may possess, we shall engage in our ends in variability, but let such variability never be led so far as to be felt despicable by these Laws, which are many times and easily recognized in Nature, such as those related to oaths or the judge we effect over our own life and that of others. Through these laws of greatest natural and moral order we shall be able to promote the greatest spirituality even further upgraded and led to levels of perfection beyond those executed solely by being spiritual, but always therefore being relative and hypocritical as the priests and scribes and today. The difference is that we do not violate any of these laws, while they claim to follow them all, while ignoring them and creating countless more.

To attain all this, we shall direct our society to in its inner jurisdictions and usual practices, allocate the needed allegories and symbolism to all these Laws and the infinite power within our spirit. Let us in our schools, guide children and teach them all these spiritual concepts, so, from a young age, we may sculpt according to our ends and we may provide them the tools to attain such a high degree of spirituality above the common adult, and even further, to such a high degree of wisdom that they, although young and seemingly innocent and weak, make their abilities and confidence, in conjunction with their spiritual powers overcome the pressures and injustices presented by any of such evil adults. Let us know and guarantee therefore, that there is no way better to lead kids to join our society or be agents of ours in third parties, than through a training from a young age, and let them be so spiritual and carefully taken care of since a young age as to make feasible for such knowledge and awakening since a young age, and to be born in a spiritual family and sense as if they were born as Taraka Brahmas, and to train since young to awaken to the truths and illusions of the matrix as if they were so most intelligent and genuinely practical among the conspiracies, so in that sense we make mold the perfect brother or agenteur for our society. Let us follow this training till the make it to our universities, and let them be so intelligent as to accomplish all this from a young age, let us further invite to our center and libraries and let read our books from a young age so the previous is more easily accomplished, and they possess such knowledge easily, opposite to the masses which we need to thoroughly deprogram after they have reached mental maturity. Let us bring this spiritual knowledge and truths of ours and of all to everyone, so wherever we go we may have a friend which may help when we are found in spiritual war with any of our enemies. Consciously or unconsciously, people will help us in such a sense and let our agents in front groups equally be found everywhere we go, and let these extensions of our society be our most prepared soldiers, above all, in spiritual terms, or at least, to minimally be so. Let us equally, in our spiritual centers and temples, in our universities, and in our learning and librarian institutions correctly and plainly preach what we practice, and inwardly, practice what we preach, so that the apparent correlates with the substantial, so that everything outside as perceives in complete trust and hence we may helped by the people whenever we may need it. Let us teach them what to do when one is attacked by these malignant forces, so that whenever we may need and we encounter one of our followers they may be able to help us or any of our agents, and let us too, teach them courage, one faculty which is needed to be enabled to fight such evil forces. Let us whenever it is possible, hire and cooperate with these spiritual persons, from birth or from practice, so that they may help us and become part of our society, and we further have between our means and even our lines, those who awakened or are since birth possessors of such spiritual aptitudes. Let us extract from society those which possess these previous qualities and those which are especially at a high degree benevolent, empathic and naturally guided towards mystic forces, so that we may possess contact and support from such strong forces of morality. Let us do the same with those which are greater practitioners of naturalism and which are great knowers of the cycles and Laws of Nature,they may further help us, in universal tones presented in the previous chapter, arrive at a better capacity to excel in such naturality, and of all these previously expressed let us direct the same towards our alumni, followers, support, agenteurs and in summary, anyone which may be related to our organization. Let us achieve all these laws and the infinite power of the spirit in conjunction with all the other principles outlined in the other chapters, and never let those interfere with these, nor these with those. So that we may find a homeostatic state where our means nor our ends justify our disruptions of the Laws, nor that these laws stagnate our path towards the consummation of the new world we desire. For all these reasons, and because such deep knowledge and understanding of the common man of our practices, we are to never lose confidence and our support of the masses, nor fear that any of our secret in such terms may be known, for none of these people (evil in their ignorance yet good otherwise)see us enemies, contrary to our enemies which are to be stoned to death if such aberrations and degenerations of theirs come to light. Thus, let us illuminate the world with our truth so that we may fear nothing and our path is illuminated in hopes of the support of the people. This will benefit us and gain us support in such deeper degrees to our enemies that, our light will be everywhere, and through these and our genuine feelings for humanity, will lead us to gain us their trust in contrary acclamation to the hate and sense of vengeance which will be gained by our enemies by the people. All this will lead our infinite power of spiritual sense and wisdom to destroy and completely shatter those of our enemies, and to gain us victory simply because of the superiority inherent to ours.

- "In the pursuit of spiritual enlightenment, we recognize the universal power within each individual, echoing the wisdom of revered figures like the saints of India, Europe, and the Middle East. Our focus lies in understanding the infinite power of the spirit, a force that emanates from the divine essence within each soul. This power, rooted in the human mind, aligns with the same force that birthed, operated, and dissolved the universe. It surpasses physical and intellectual prowess, asserting its dominance through spiritual progress.
- We distinguish ourselves by embracing a unique perception that transcends conventional rationalization and visualization. This heightened awareness allows us to explore other realms, dimensions, and realities, fostering spiritual evolution and deeper understanding. Our enlightened state leads us to be more tolerant, breaking free from the limited perspectives that trap the masses in fear, lack of ideals, and mediocrity.
- To harness this profound power of the mind and spirit, we delve into the scientific exploration of spirituality, demystifying practices with reason instead of succumbing to superstition and dogma. Our erudition extends to the intricate knowledge of yoga, Sanskrit, and the spiritual sciences prevalent in India. By mastering these disciplines, we empower ourselves to counteract the dark forces of black magic and understand the entities invoked by our adversaries.
- In our pursuit of spiritual perfection, we go beyond the limitations of specific religions, embracing a universal approach. Our deep understanding encompasses emotional, concentrational, and idealizational intricacies, ensuring a holistic perspective that integrates seamlessly with scientific exploration.
- As practitioners of spiritual arts, we utilize practical methods such as meditation, oration, and visualization. We delve into the scientific relations between emotion, wisdom, allegories, and the human body and brain, seeking the path to liberation from the cycles of birth and rebirth. Yet, in our journey, we maintain simplicity and practicality, allowing us to approach the eternal with a clear and rational mind.
- Guided by the Laws of Creation, which we equate with the Laws of Nature, our principles revolve around spirituality, naturality, and morality. Upholding these absolute laws, we navigate the complexities of human conduct with unwavering dedication.

- To disseminate our profound knowledge, we initiate spiritual education from a young age, sculpting young minds into beacons of enlightenment. By nurturing spiritual families and imparting our wisdom, we ensure a continuous flow of awakened individuals who align with our cause.
- In our interactions with society, we strive to illuminate the truth without fear, gaining the trust and support of the masses. Our light outshines the darkness cast by our adversaries, as our infinite spiritual wisdom prevails, ensuring victory through inherent superiority."

6. History, present and prophecy

Study history to control the future | Utilize covert means and front-societies for artifact analysis | Spiritual faculties aid in uncovering truths about historical objects. | Digitalize and analyze findings using artificial intelligence | Handle prophecies discreetly, considering moral impact. | Infiltrate indigenous groups covertly for collaboration. | Learn from despots of the past to transmute negativity | Use spirituality for moral guidance in historical pursuits | Interiorize knowledge for privacy and enemy ignorance | Consequences for immoral acts fall on those skipping morality | Collaborate with native people for mutual respect and benefit

There is no better way to foretell the future and the deeds by which we may be our enemies, through the intricacies employed by the same, than by studying history. In studying history, and acquiring through all kinds of means in possibility and predisposition to our resources we shall be better equipped to confront the future and the many difficulties that we nevertheless shall face at what point or the other. The past is but we shall only utilize our energy in searching and directing our means to what is rather rational and most probable to have really happened or to the truest of facts and proves that such an event has happened. Contrary to such facts, we cannot study in any way any of the opinions exerted by the scribes of that time, especially on spiritual and religious manners, because it is within the most probable that what they have described is a completely distortion of the truth with the object of hiding our true history and the true history of most if not all of our origin as human beings. Therefore, we shall employ all kinds of methods to prove through concrete evidence that this or that event has really happened that way, and to decide, upon obtaining such evidence, if it shall be uncovered to the public.

We ought to find, found and fund front-societies for the study of the past, such as archeological, antiquarian, anthropological and other societies of such kind. They shall be camouflage from our enemies so that we have any relation with them as possible, let them be found in any country without any connection between them and us. Let us whenever we have an opportunity, infiltrate them certain group of population all over the planet, especially those of indigenous nature, with our agents and build such centers for their benefit, and for the protection of these antiquities, in such a manner, that they shall always only perceive their benefit, and our enemy shall not even know that we are behind it, without any of them deducing that the most benefited among people on Earth are us. Let us build such societies whenever possible within the Laws of the country, and whenever such societies are not permitted, let us proceed to have our agents search for such antiquities and evidences of the past through converted private means, so no one ever seeks to know that we are the ones behind such extraction of this historic facts. Let us have these private agents seem and infiltrate as if they were the poorest and most common among all men, so that not one person dares to find any connection between them and the extraction of such evidence nor they're subordination to our orders. Therefore, let it be preferable that this person ought to be a single adult, who has the greatest capacity to hide such evidence and find no confrontation with any other person. For in such a society, whenever there is more than one person, there is always confrontation, if both of these are not in the same mental alignment. Therefore, let such agents of history of us be mono-idealistic and only perceive and do what we tell them to do through our third-agents. After we have created such front groups and placed such agents, let such agents be the most knowledgeable and train and order them to study the history and places where such historic evidence may be found, and let us provide them with the resources and mediums by which such extraction of historical objects is to be consummated. Then let us decide, if such should be keep hidden in our secret places and mediums, or if we should display them to the public through third-party museums, let us, if such our displayed to the public, to the display them in the same museums our enemies have built for such objects, so that they are the ones which to need to be questioned on the precedence and extraction of such data from the native people, and not us. Let us, in previous reference, take such resources without anyone knowing, not even the native people, for in so doing we will not be labeled as thieves but merely as historians and extractors of nature which is universal and open to us. Let us through covert or overt means have these indigenous collaborate with us, so these accusations so commonly everted are diminished, and let us share such findings with them, in contraposition to the usurpation without care effectuated by our enemies. Let us therefore, in so providing and collaborating with them, provide further impossibilities to our enemy, that, in case of seeking for the artifacts as us, will, if so doing, usurp the same from the native people, by such means, when usurping the native people, they are usurping us, and when people accuse them of abusing such aboriginals they shall be accused of abusing us, by which we shall defend our indigenous brothers and sisters, and therefore, have further means and justifications to assert a sentential strike against our enemy, without anyone knowing that such or such groups our working for our ends and that we have created such false-flag or pretext by which our attacks and competition in violents terms with our enemies is justified. Let us, therefore, whenever we do this through the indigenous people, be public and known to everyone so that we may be hidden under the camouflage and pretexts provided by the same, and that when such is done by solitary agents, be covert, so that we are not found to have been the ones behind such secret extraction of antiquities, and that if such a thing is found, that it shall later be justified through all kinds of moral ambiguities we may find within the fulfilling of the Laws of Creation, and placing always the end as superior in helping such or such people than to the so-called immoral means denoted by the fanatic moralists, which do not take into account the situation and many ramifications of charity by which such an extraction may take, in contrast as if it was gathered by our enemies.

Let us finally when being in possession of such antiquities and texts of the ancients time, analyze us with through all the knowledge and references we have gathered in our "Knowledge is power" protocol, so that we may find the relations throughout all this vast data between the information and intricacies found within this and those found within the other. Let us especially utilize this occult knowledge which is uncommon to the common man and labeled as a conspiracy, but of which we know it is true, that it shall further serve to understand such texts and antiquities. Let us always digitalize such findings and through artificial intelligence find any relations between this and the data, and the truth may be further uncovered. Let us effectuate such operations through our inner-society experts and erudites of history, or let us utilize third-party agents which shall be skilled at such compromises and which at all times be directed by us in the same methods. Upon obtaining such information, we shall further decide if the public is apt to acquire or the methods by which we shall transmit, and further we shall utilize such information, if it so deems it, to obtain prophecies upon which we may discover what is to happen in the future, what are the prophets, the saviors and the people, other than us, that shall change this world for the better. We may obtain even more data about places to which we shall go and continue to find more and more information, leading to more and more patterns and prophecies by which the complete truth shall be revealed to us. This information shall preferably be stored in computers which are based in no network and which shall be digitalized but only through our own means so they can never be checked and hacked by our enemies. Let us further, when transmitting such antiquity, do it sublimely, so that people may recognize that truth through indirect means, let us create pseudo-authors and museums, cultural centers and more, created by ourselves, in which we shall display such evidence in the past covertly and people may awaken to their true origin.

Let us especially, persecute those texts which speak of prophecy and relate to all those conspiracies and information as to how our enemy works, that we may utilize such information to further our means and ends, and so the path to this new world is more clearly shown to us. Let us, when in knowledge of such prophecy, correctly relate ourselves to the place of unfoldment or the people involved in the prophecy in such a way that they do not know that we are either blocking such a prophet or prophecy or letting it further develop with our support. If the prophecy is against us, or, which is seldom the case, we shall revoke it by improving and changing the causes, especially of a psychic and spiritual principle, as to revert this prophecy in our favor. In studying the future we will better understand what were the principles of those ancient civilizations which we seek to imitate, such as Ancient Atlantis and Lemuria. Especially let us have all the information regarding Lemuria, for this is the civilization which stands above all others as an example to humanity of what we shall be like in the future, and how our society is to be directed. Let us learn the intricacies of the worst and most cruel of the despots of the past, so we learn how to transmute such possible expression of the same in the current society, so we may further help the people get out of such mistakes which have been so many times reproduced in the history of mankind. Let us turn them, from their dark self, invoked in this age of Kali Yuga, to the shiny self, invoked in the past by these civilizations, and by which ideals we shall, through whatever moral means possible, conduct the lives of these people we are to change and train. We ought to pay special attention to these prophecies when it comes to these youngsters, and to train them for the correct finalization of these prophecies from a young age. Let us prepare them in all kinds of arts and means and resources formed by our own so we can protect this prophecy from unfolding the way it should be, without our enemies accomplishing their ends of precisely ending the same prophecies. But let those involved in the prophecies, better remain unknown to the people and only get such a fame when the time has precisely come to acquire it, and when the end of secrecy regarding their existence is appropriate for the unfolding of the same. Let us have contact and means by which to contact the secret agents of our enemy through converted means, through which we can acquire the knowledge and present and past texts on the future and the plans of these. Let them give us hints as to where such or such information may be found and where our enemies hide the objects of the prophecies or even the people which they may control mentally and sequester, let us save such people from their subordination and provide them the appropriate help by which we shall further destroy our enemies. All these agents and knowers of the past, which have been ex- this or ex-that, regarding the top spheres and experiments of our enemies, be also known to us and to contact them without them knowing that they are providing such information (whenever such a method is possible or otherwise) and if they know to convince them that we are the ones which are better equipped to further this prophecy, and to find the connection between us and them, to create the holistic prophecy which leads to the new world. In such temporal dichotomies and intricacies we may find what we ought to do in the exact moment it shall be effectuated. Let us further constitute our means in relation to these places, objects and people which are in relation to ourselves or the prophecies which must be manifested upon this world.

Let us further utilize the spirituality of ourselves and all are agents with the objects of finding, through this cosmic intuition, the events of the past and the future. Whenever we may feel undecided about the nature of past events or of objects and their history, let us through our own abilities or that of our agents of such kind, address the true origin of these objects, abilities such as psychometric, clairvoyance, and clairsentience or any of these kind, shall be directed towards the discovery of the truth regarding the origin, events and other factors of historic nature regarding these. Through these means of spiritual kind may be utilized in all phases of the antiquarian method. When seeking such antiques, we shall utilize visions and other extra-sensorial intuitional faculties to find the place where they may be found. When obtaining the object or prophecy, let us use some more specialized of these mediums to obtain the meaning and purpose of such objects and the connection it had with such an event, so we may more easily visualize what event it may be related to. Then, when acquiring it, let us further, spirituality, study if the people are ready to receive and what are the people involved in the prophecy or who are those who have the most relation with these objects and the events or prophecies they lead to. Let us, through such spiritual means, do what we ought to do, whenever possible, with no label or entity placed upon our mission, for in such a way, no one, except ourselves, will acquire such knowledge about the location of such objects, the meanings and prophecies they lead to. Through such interiorization of knowledge and the means by which we are led to the same, we may better cover our means and missions, and it may further be used when it is so important, and when we prefer to effectuate such antiquarian method in greater privacy and the people, and somehow our enemies, which lack such spiritual powers, remain ignorant, in their own benefit, of this knowledge and events they may not be benefitted by. This antiquarian objects and the prophecies they lead to may only be uncovered when the result of the same is not immoral or leads to the destruction of our society, or to the death of people, otherwise, we may let more or less people receive such information in the manner it is appropriate in the aforementioned factors. Whenever such information or antiques are robbed, let them be known to the people, or otherwise, let our enemy feel our wrath for committing such immoral acts. But let the consequences fall only upon those which skip morality, namely, our enemies, and those which are of greater importance to ignorance and to our desire to uncover the truth and help these native people we should give fairly as they deserve, and let us always learn from them and to always treat with the maximum respect whenever possible, and let us always collaborate with them and persuade to join our society or front-groups, so in such a way we may extract such information and objects without be accused of robbery by our enemies, by natives, nor by Nature and her laws.

- "Study history to anticipate the future and confront challenges. Use covert means to fund front-societies for past studies. Infiltrate indigenous groups for collaboration, maintaining secrecy. Establish private agents to extract historical evidence discreetly. Collaborate with indigenous people, sharing findings and providing benefits.

- Use spiritual faculties like psychometry and clairvoyance in historical pursuits. Digitalize and analyze artifacts using AI. Consider morality in handling prophecies and historical knowledge. Create front-societies within legal bounds, fund archeological, anthropological studies. Keep connections covert, build centers globally for benefit, conceal involvement.

- Train knowledgeable agents for historical studies, decide on public display or secrecy. Take resources discreetly, collaborate with indigenous people, defend against accusations. Analyze acquired antiquities using occult knowledge and digitalize findings. Transmit information sublimely, create cultural centers for public awakening. Utilize spiritual intuition for events of the past and future.

- Address the true origin of objects using psychometric and clairvoyant abilities. Use spiritual means in all phases of antiquarian methods. Seek antiques through visions and extra-sensorial faculties. Study the meaning and purpose of objects through specialized mediums. Conduct spiritual studies without labels for privacy.

- Ensure consequences for immoral acts fall on those lacking morality, not on native people. Collaborate with natives respectfully, extract information without accusations. Uncover antiquarian objects and prophecies morally, avoiding harm to society. Learn from and help native people, treating them with respect and fairness."

7. The political question

In the pursuit of spiritual progress, we challenge political and economic corruption, urging leaders to prioritize humanity. | Interfering peacefully, we guide them toward morality and spirituality, fostering societal growth. | Eliminating sinister influence involves exposing secret groups for justice and equality. | Guiding leaders includes training in oratory and theater, shaping moral beacons for positive transformation. | Judicious intervention assesses politicians based on deeds, paving the way for justice-aligned leaders. | Revolutionary change uses movements to reshape constitutions for universal fairness. | Combatting shadowy influence involves indirect war on secretive groups, using strategic and flexible power. | Spiritual consciousness transmutes political forces through transcendent methods, infusing lasting transformation. | Strategic training educates future leaders for societal awakening, shaping an enlightened legacy. | Flexibility and vastness allow us to be covert or overt, directing political powers through consciousness and providence.

Politics and economics would be of no concern to the awakened people if it was not certain that politicians and so-called magnates do not bear in their interest the quality of life and spiritual progress of humanity, but that they are the first one, and most indulgent in such interference in the liberties of the people, and, at the same time, in ours. This interference would have not be a problem to society and ourselves, if it was not of a sinister and immoral nature, but as it only beneficiary are their implementers, they consolidate those in power and hence do not bring a fair system in which justice and equality, within the principles of logic and practicality, is to be found. Such society and modus operandi is contrary to our way of seeing life and to our idea of how society shall develop to bring the most out of every human, especially in the spiritual arena. Therefore, whenever such is the case, we will have no option but to interfere in the same, to bring it back to morality, naturality and spirituality and to stop the leaders from affecting the lives of people to such a high degree. Such interference will at most times be of a peaceful nature, without us having to allocate our own lives for the end of such turmoil, but to always, whenever possible, use third parties for the fulfillment of the same. The question, above all, is one of reason and balance, for the fulfillment of the state of awakening we want in society. If such awakening is not occurring given the acts of the politicians or those behind the same, why shall we trust them to fulfill their mission? If their objects are contrary to our objects (which are the universal and spiritual objects which will lead to perfection in human life) and contrary to the dignity of human life, what other option do we have but to exterminate, one way or the other? Therefore, let us have no other option but to interfere in such events, secretly or covertly, and to do so whenever it is against humanity and its natural rights. The following method we ought to follow to respond to such interference in the dignity of humanity and its awakening and spiritual progress:

Let us not judge politicians according to the system in which they are developed, but let us judge each politician according to their acts and desire they may want to bring to the people, if such desires are evil, shall we deny them continuance in their government, if such desires are good, but they are not fulfilled, let us give them a second opportunity in which they will have to follow our instruction and follow our orders, given that they cannot follow the laws of nature, let us present them the same to do. If a politician has evil desires and evil acts, let us exterminate them through our agents, for they have no right to continue even in their existence, for their lives have affected the lives of thousands of millions of people, and by such numbers, their termination if justified. If a politician has good intentions but they are deranged given his inaptitude, let us also give him a second opportunity, but one in which they only can have good motives and good acts. This is given to a question of politicians individually,but the problem of politics is the political system involves many people, and one may take the role of the other, or one may facilitate or interfere with the intentions and acts of the other. Our judgment of such politicians within a greater political system within that country and their inter-relation, shall be judged according to their alignment with the Laws of Creation found within the logics of the All, and if the same are seeking the awakening of the people. Given the degree to which they may misalign or align with such concepts we may take lighter or graver actions against their persona or the various personas which are of the same nature. Sometimes such people are simply, given their low intellect or smartness in such situations, unable to fulfill their good intentions. In such a case, and whenever their intentions are genuine, let us help such people with supporting agents which may covertly guide them towards the right path, all which may secretly presented and directed by us, and by which we may test if such or such system is to work, and always with the intent of not destroying the or experimenting with the people, but of doing it softly and within such moral demarcations.

Sometimes, it is not the politicians themselves, but the political system and the many retardations provided by its constitution permeated by inadequacies and illogical methodologies which are to be changed. In such instances we ought to change the prescription given in the constitution or political system of that country. This change is a tremendously difficult one, for the whole government and the politicians to overturn or persuade into such a change of constitution must be effectuated, and this seems almost as if it was an impossibility. We may, first, present such changes to the highest in government, which, if not in accordance, will have to feel the wrath, not of us, but of the people. For this we will have to awaken more and more people to the defects of such a political system, and let them ask the politicians why they are not open to subscribe to this new government, why shall they not change it for the one which is right for them? Let us change the opinion of such people, let us create new ideologies, movements and pressures groups within the country which are to be changed, and to guide them to our ends without them even knowing that they do so, thanks to the guidance provided by us to them through our agents and front-groups, especially those of young idealistic people who want a change, and who will effectuate such revolution necessary to update the constitution for us. Let us, especially, construct these movements thanks to the guidance of young men who are especially apt at taking arms and evoking their wrath against such people. But let us not forget, that we may also use young women to create this movements and any other of such young and marginalized and of such people who may want a change from such defectuous form of government, let us provide them, with our front-groups and third-party agents, with the tools, ideological, psychic, spiritual and more of such kind, to bring about such revolution and change in the governance and its forms and methods of acting and oppressing the people, or being inefficient in providing such natural right to all humans. By this revolution we create devolution, or return the power to the people, the righteous people who are to perform the best in moral, natural and spiritual terms for the progress of the nation, and create evolution, for in this we are giving the people are spiritual practices through all kinds of overt and covert means, and their path towards the infinite is further shortened and brought to life thanks to our interference in such events. This is all due to the inept and lack of humility of this same politicians, to rationalize what is best for their people, what is best for the progres of the people, and therefore, that if they do not change with our transmutative methods, they shall do it by the iron hammer of the people. They should have been humble and have kept their ego at bay given such faults, but as they do not recognize the same, they will recognize the need of the people, and of us in our support and guidance, to terminate and overturn such faults within the very system affects the life of all, and obfuscates their spiritual and wisdom progress.

For the fulfillment of these previously explained in relation to the politicians and the government, we may utilize any of these methods:

- Use spies, agents and others, individually or through font groups to pressure the politicians to change their policies, let us take many forms and be the journalist, the workers, the cook or any other profession which may let us have close contact with them.
- Use, when such a process is necessary, mercenaries to finally take the life of such people given that they so deserve it, effectuate through all types of means, and be sure to always use agents, but to never do such acts ourselves.
- If we need to change the government and constitution altogether, we may do so by equally convince and pressuring the politicians which have so legislative powers, or we may conjunctly persuade all of them to create such changes, let us equally utilize agents and other which may pressure politicians to create such change in the constitution whenever it is so required.
- Let us, if politicians do not listen to our prospects, create ideologies, movements, and other pressure and revolutionary groups directed at pointing out the many faults of government and the ways in which they need to change, and to eventually effectuate such termination thanks to the military and resources of other kinds provided by us, and let these men be especially in contact or plainly in the military, so such resources are more easily attained and the change can take place easily.
- Let us use the power of social media and other such platforms of communication, physically or digitally, to create such groups or movements with our agents, let them do all types of rites in our guidance without they knowing that we are behind it, so they may prepare with complete secrecy and spiritual manners the change in the state and the change in the constitution in the country, so a change which starts within the very energies of ethereal nature changes the country towards the right path without us having to guide such revolutionary process.

Such processes we may execute if the problem is found in the outer layers of government and constitution, in the politicians which hold such seats, but I fear that problem is rather found in the secret groups that create the conspiracies and prospects for such politicians and policies to develop in such a manner. These are our enemies which direct everything from the shadows, and who, through all kinds of tricks and methods, give orders and create conspiracies in such countries to direct in the way they so desire. Let us therefore, develop all kinds of methods of war, direct or indirect, overtly or secretly against these groups in the shadows and let us obstruct their interference in politics, not so much by attacking the politicians which they secretly control, but by directing our scolds against them, by locating and analyzing their ways and methods, into the development of such constitutions and politicians, and to so, through all types of hidden means, convert to our ways, bring them to propose our proposals to such politicians and to stubborn (in a positive sense), to our policies, that such case and positive transmutation does not take place, we shall have to obstruct their powers upon the politicians, and if such same obstruction is not possible, we shall have no other option but to eliminate such agents or eliminating the society from which such agents and control over the politicians is developed. Let us for such objects, especially utilize our front-groups and any of such which create such ideologies directed at eliminating or hating such secrets or discrete groups, and to direct the rage of the people at them, so we do not have to move a finger, but all is done by the people which we awaken, which in such awakening process to the true nature of such societies, which, in turn, are our enemies, exert over them the wrath and righteous spirit of the people against such immoral and unfair groups. Let us through the people, especially those in the awakening process who engage and indulge in such conspiracy against these groups, take arms and renew or destroy them when such a case is so necessary for the progress of humanity as a whole. Let us through them, are awakening agents, our military agents, and all of such agents and front groups, and movements, direct their attention or wrath at them through the one located closest to such societies and their strongholds, so their termination or centers of powers are diminished and so is their political power. Let us, as we know of such arts, create front-groups of the spiritual kind to direct their attacks against them, and to impregnate their temples and lodges of such energy contrary to the one invoked by them, so all their premises and objects are confronted when such response is equally needed. Our numbers and theirs are very minute in comparison to the people, who are many times greater in number than them and us. Therefore, we have nothing to fear from the people, for we are to always support and receive their sympathy. But they are ones, given their evil acts, to have the most fear of the people and the wrath which shall be directed at their many evil intentions. We know that they control the military and police, but such forces are rendered meaningless for we equally hold power over them, and such power is directed precisely, at our enemies, whenever they utilize this same power to abuse the people. We know for certain that our enemies may create such same methods and groups to be directed at us, and to persuade the ignorant people to hate us, in such a sense and in such a state of slumber in the most of the society we may be in disadvantage, but we know equally how to influence the psyche of the people, and we know that the truth and the good, shal always deceive their deceptive and immoral means and objects. For such, let us equally have no option but utilize all our powers and secret methods and tricks, which are in accordance with the laws of all and the secret powers of nature, to destroy all of such deceptions and evil intentions through all kinds of means against us. Such disease which is at all times created in society by them against us, in their fear that we awaken the people to the truth, shall be brought ineffective and shattered by our many agents, knowledge and analysis, through spiritual and psychic powers of their innermost intentions and places of hide, so we may render them ineffective before they are executed. In the, as stated in the first chapter, this is a battle between truth vs deception and of knowledge vs ignorance. Therefore, let us always, and at all times, bring the people more and more information of their evil deeds that they have brought deceits about us and the truth we expose on them and the many deceptions they have planted in the minds of these people. Let the people discern who is truly evil, and let them be guided out of such slumber by knowledge, wisdom and truth, factors by which they will prefer us before them. Let us for such turn of events, whenever it may occur, take many forms and many faces so that they never know, given their vast ignorance, who they are attacking, and let us be our enemy as we are ourselves, so that we may know more of them than they know of us, and the people know more of them in truthfulness and they know of their deception against us, so that whenever they may unconsciously attack us, they in the same unconscious manner attack them. Let us not unfairly judge such people within our enemies, for may so be unfairly judged by them or the people, thus we shall always give to these what they deserve, and give the people, unconscious after all, what they deserve given our agents and to with, whatever moral and smooth means possible, direct their possible wrath and oblivious indulgence in their lies, to them, through a change in their consciousness and final discernment of who truly needs to be usurped from society. Let us be our enemy, or let our enemy unconsciously benefit us, whenever they plan such secret plans against us, so that whenever they may want to bring a revolution against us, they bring a revolution against themselves, so that whenever they insist in continuing their power over the lives of people, such power is transmuted in the right ways, and their secret connection and many evil intentions towards politics and us, is directed is diffused in our benefit and the benefit of the people. Therefore, let us ultimately be so flexible and so vast that it means our always secret whenever and wherever they may so need to be, or totally overt and masculine whenever they may so need to be masculine. So that we are not recognized everywhere, and our power is kept alive at all times, as a flame which is always directed at the enemy without retardation. Let us always, direct such political powers and our enemies in relation to such power, through our utmost instrument, that of consciousness, spirituality and providence, which is so tremendous and all-mighty and perfect in its reasons and methods, that it will be impossible to break, for we will always know more of them that they will every know of us, for we will have spiritual powers in the side of light which they shall never enjoy, and for we will have the benefit of God and truth by our side, and this power is above them, the ignorance of the people, the evils of the politicians, and in short, capable of destroying and transmuting all such everted by these, their demons and their agents.

Sometimes, we ourselves shall be like the enemy if we have no other option to direct such forces through our own front-groups. Let us train these possible politicians and movement since young from our educational and cultural institutions, let us do so us needed so that, if there is vacancy and the people lack guidance within such or such nation, they may be guided to the light of God, and so that they may be guided by such agents who shall have as their sole object that of bringing such nations to a better path and to utilize all such means to create the ideals and to awaken the people to new realities, for this, let us train them in oratory, theater and whatever other forms by which they may penetrate the psyche of people, and awake to the new alignments in accordance with the perfection presented by our model of government, which shall ultimately guide the whole of humanity to this new spiritual world we desire and which shall be maintained over the longer term given this new state of consciousness once and for all injected in the minds of people, who are finally open to new realities and know the truth and many truths, leading to the pinnacle of wisdom.

- In our pursuit of spiritual progress, we confront political and economic corruption, urging leaders to prioritize humanity. Our peaceful interference guides leaders toward morality, naturality, and spirituality, fostering societal growth. To eliminate sinister influence, we expose secret groups and obstruct their machinations for justice and equality.

- Guiding leaders involves oratory and theater training, shaping moral beacons for positive transformation. Judicious intervention assesses politicians based on deeds, paving the way for justice-aligned leaders. Revolutionary change utilizes movements to reshape constitutions for universal fairness.

- Combatting shadowy influence involves indirect war on secretive groups, using strategic and flexible power. Spiritual consciousness transmutes political forces through transcendent methods, infusing lasting transformation. Strategic training educates future leaders for societal awakening, shaping an enlightened legacy.

- Flexibility allows us to be covert or overt, always directing political powers through the instrument of consciousness and providence. Politics and economics concern awakened people when politicians prioritize self-interest over humanity. Interference in liberties becomes problematic when of sinister nature, consolidating power without justice or equality.

- Our intervention aims to bring society back to morality, naturality, and spirituality, countering leaders' negative impact. This interference is mostly peaceful, utilizing third parties whenever possible. The key is reason and balance for societal awakening.

- We judge politicians based on deeds and intentions, exterminating those with evil desires. Good-intentioned politicians receive a second opportunity with guidance. Change may involve altering constitutions, and we use various methods to pressure and persuade politicians.

- Sometimes the problem lies in the political system, requiring a difficult change in the constitution. Movements for change involve presenting new ideologies, creating pressure groups, and guiding revolutions covertly. The aim is to devolve power back to the people and bring about societal evolution.

- The battle extends to secret groups manipulating politics. We employ various methods to obstruct their interference, utilizing front-groups and agents. Through the people, we direct attention and wrath toward these groups, aiming to diminish their power.

- In responding to attacks and deceptions, we expose truth through information dissemination. We take many forms, remaining flexible and vast, ensuring our enemies unconsciously benefit us. Our ultimate instrument is consciousness, spirituality, and providence, guided by the light of God.

- In certain situations, we train politicians and movements aligned with our ideals from a young age. Through oratory and theater training, we shape agents capable of guiding nations toward a better path. This educational and cultural influence ensures alignment with our model of government, ultimately leading humanity to spiritual enlightenment and wisdom.

8. The economic question

Embrace spiritual ideals over economics | Build an ideology beyond economic necessity | Grow detached from artificial economic prospects | Develop holistic economic systems through intellectual means | Infiltrate, collapse, offer alternatives | Execute actions with humility and detachment | Base existence on spiritual wealth | Avoid dependency on artificial economic systems | Create stable, fair, non-monetary economic systems | Influence people subtly through economic change | Infiltrate enemies, collapse their systems and transmutate their evil | Marginalize enemies economically through people's support | Experiment with alternative economic systems secretly | Guide society to commune with the All | Evolve without limiting ourselves economically | Seek universal presence, wisdom, and goodness | Embrace infinite possibilities with God's guidance.

As important as the political question is the economic question, for it bears a profound influence in the maintenance of our society and its means to awaken people and construct the world we want. This question holds a close relation with the political question, for it may be the politicians which usurp our economy, especially those concerned with the economic questions and those especially professing socialist unfair economic systems. But if our society would bear its existence solely upon the economic question, it would surely collapse, for economics is to, at any point, as it is so now constructed in this society, collapse, and lead to misery and poverty. This we do not want. Therefore, let our movement, our entity as a group, extend beyond such economic "necessity", which is not a necessity except in the so constructed principles of such a materialistic society. This we may change by changing the politico-economic system as presented in the previous chapter, but just as this is risky, it is risky to not be risky under such constantly-evolving systems, for this would only lead to our death, for so it is given in such a society. Hence let the existence of our society not depend upon such artificially constructed economic prospects, but let us extend beyond as long as we do not control the politico-economic system, let us withstand all such falls by bringing a movement which would always bear in existence, and which would beyond any of such economic or material deficiencies, let too, our ideals not be based upon such economics, but such economic based upon our ideals, let our ideals and the social expansion of our society be both our means and our objects, and let our resources and economy be solely an instrument to take into effect and reach the aforementioned. For we stand as a universal family in the most difficult of situations and artificially imposed situations by those who seek to control our lives through such aberrant means. Let us stand beyond such aberration, beyond such meaningless materialism. Let all our actions be executed with utter humility and knowledge of its ephemeral nature, so the more we rest detached from such materials, the more we renew ourselves and prosper beyond the same. It is not about being rich or poor, but of being that which we ought to be to be in accordance with the prosperity of such time and place, and to which it naturally conducts itself within such an environment, and at the same time towards Gods. Different societies, in different degrees of technological evolution may be rich in different ways, one may be content with food, while the other may need more to fill their desires and reactions. But what stands beyond such wealth, is the spiritual wealth, which is the true progress and which is maintained beyond our death, and that of our body. We shall, for such a reason, bear our existence not upon material riches, but upon spiritual ones, so the legacy left by us may never die., and hence the existence of our society may not be based upon something which is temporal in nature, but upon God's eternal lap and legacy. Our movement, our ideals, our *raison d'être* in its innermost nature, remains free from all delusion and stands within and therein, in the souls and minds of people, contrary to the "out-there" and without which is professed by the our enemies, which portray to seek one thing while searching the other. For this same reasonings, let us not bear our existence upon economies, but let us modify and transcend the same in the instrumentalization of our purpose and the attainment of, precisely, what Mother Earth and the whole of Creation desires, let us be based upon eternal laws and not upon the such crude economic and mundane phenomena. The spiritual power we possess, extends beyond any of such economic power, for one is sure to pass away, while the other remains and stands tall beyond any of such adversities. We will possess many resources, but these resources may only be utilized for the betterment of planet Earth and the awakening of people. Let us stand and camouflage beyond any of the greedy appropriations and unnecessary encompassment of our enemy, let us be all resources to all humans, let us be the means by which people are to be given a better life, so our destruction in economic terms means the destruction of them. Let us be the center by which a new futuristic economic system, which is more fair may be developed, let us develop such holistic economic systems, and given the spoken on the previous chapter, presented to the people together with our spiritual practices, so that they may grow so much fervor and favor for our cause that its change for that of our enemies will bear a profound discontent upon the people, let us not be attached to these, but bear its existence upon the spiritual, so our economic system, with the lamp of truth and practicality, may come back stronger in counteraction to that exposed by our enemies. The ideals of our enemies exist upon the materio-economic question, our spiritual means and objects transcend this very economic question, and hence it is the materio-economic question which responds to our ideals. For, how can the spiritual respond to the material, when it is the latter which provides it with life and color? So how can our enemies withstand our spiritual fervor, if it is this, that precisely asks for that which they bear and presented to the people as being the sole object of the aforementioned. Our spirit, our truth which stands upon universal principles and laws, stands beyond the disappearance of the universe and the 7 great ages, how can the same, therefore, not extend beyond the greediness and injustices given by some meaningless, purposeless and pathetic humans which call themselves entitled of such resources above all of humanity, if they are so minute in number and so contrary to the eternal which we ourselves promulgate as no one else does? For this reasons, our name, our power, our resources, are nothing but secondary traits by which we seek to destroy ignorance and our enemies, so these our always instruments of our ideology, in her means and objects, and not to be attached or dependent upon them, for in such we would ultimately be led to the same death that our enemies push to the people and bear upon themselves in some kind of masochist existence and desire for the dead, for that which lacks life and gives nothing to life. Let our ideology therefore bear spiritual reaches above all else, and let all other reaches be based upon this, so they are given life, light and reason, and they sustain our resources beyond the many changes which are to occur in the world and society given its changing nature.

We will create, through our schools, cultural and learning centers, and many others of such kind, economic systems which will be so practical and superior to the ones presented by our enemies, that people will not accept living without them. Let his economic system be stable, and if possible, eliminate the influence of money and all monetary concepts and factors from society, so we can live beyond money. For money is solely intended to limit and enslave society. Let us present, economic systems, that if monetary, presente such solidity and are so stable, that they are not prone to the ups and downs of the current economic systems, and that they may be so efficient in sufficiently providing the minimum to live for all, that believing in anything else will live to the rage and wrath of the people, which in that case may be directed against the economic system implemented by our enemies. In this economic system we may better protect our entities and we may sustain such change through rationality and spirituality. Let our enemies always find enticing promoting their systems, for as long as they do we will surpass in such effects, and ours will receive the support of the people. Let people support our economic cause, but never let it be known to them that they do, that we are the ones behind such new and revolutionary economic ideologies which we may further put in practice through our political and military means. Whenever our enemies may have the idea of imposing some of these immoral and materialistic economic system to destroy society, to lead to misery, poverty and humiliation, let us use our resources, especially the military, the technological, the spiritual to destroy them, and let our word lead to the empowerment of the people upon hearing it, let them be motivated by our systems, let them take arms directed by us to seek this new system, and let them do so naturally and unconsciously yet subconsciously, so such changes which are taken over without overthinking are rendered to our cause and to the termination of those systems imposed by our enemies. The further question is that our enemies may always try to impose such systems upon our lives, and especially wherever we may have some kind of influence or benefit for the people, but as our system is based upon the spiritual, we will rise again beyond any of such privations of liberty, and liberty and dignity will be refreshed by our powers which supersede their mere materialistic and psychopathics means and objects.

Let us, from time to time, and whenever and wherever such is the case, as means to maintain ourselves and our legacy, in conjunction with our spiritual riches, beyond time, space and person, as we recollect when we are in samadhi state, execute precisely that which our enemies pretend to do: help the poor and marginalized. As so stated in previous chapter, if we are capable of providing that help through genuine means, and if we are able (we surely will), of fulfilling the promises which are enemies do not fulfill, we will have the support of those they deceive, and hence the unconscious followers of our enemies will become our allies, for in both the right and the left, they will see in us what they have not seen in them. We know that methods of our enemy, that of dividing people into frameworks by which they may easily put them both into battle with the other, are reflected in the faults of such systems, and they provide the problem and the solution when any of such events happen. In such a way they maintain people in artificial confrontation with the other, while never fully fulfilling, similar to the religions that endlessly speak of God but never really indulge in any spiritual practices. Society is thus led by our enemies in constant problems and delusions, while they pretend to provide solutions, which are always nothing but this same delusion time and time again. People are in such slumber that they are not capable of discerning and realizing that they have been defrauded time and time again, and have been providing with limiting materialistic ideologies which never fully provides them a solution to their material and spiritual problems, but which solely maintains them between the bad and the not so bad. We are the ones who shall wake them up, as we have already done, and bring them out of such state by making them realizing the dualistic and confrontational tactics of our enemies, by our own power and presence of efficiency in the true alternative presented by us, making them realize that our system is far superior to the one presented by our enemy. That our system is presented with good intentions, and that our system takes into account the spiritual nature of humankind, its liberty, its dignity and its morality or laws, and that in such a manner, it is preferable to them to support our system than to defend theirs. *Eo ipso*, our system will be preferable to that of our enemies, and those who in slumber support the plans of our enemies will support our plans, and turn from a lack of consciousness, a state of comfort full of mediocrity and limitations, will be contrasted with one of expansion of consciousness, in a state of continuous betterment and possibilitation of impossibility. Let us affect any of these which may be more conceivable and efficient for us in such instances, and either build a movement from those who are so delusional and abused that they have no other hope, except us, and let us further give them such hope by exterminating our enemies in their evoking of such objects and immoral control over the people.

In such sense we may even infiltrate our enemies, and we utilize their methods against themselves, by confronting ones with the other, and growing in them a seed of delusion and hopelessness in the economic systems they support, by which us, applying their own means, terminate with the existence of their resources, and hence the continuance of their society must be led under the guidance of our economic system and not their. Let us infiltrate and secretly persuade to put our system into practice, and so in doing it, they may never pretend to effectuate to make our system look bad, but let us when such is the case rapidly inform the people, and if the people are in such slumber, we will have no option but to operate under fatal means and consequences against these enemies of ours. For our enemies like to distort the truth through their luciferian inversion, but let us show the proof everywhere in such raw state, that finally the power of discernment of the people, especially those most apt to so being and to take against against these, will be stronger than the tactics used by our enemies. Let them be destroyed by their own ideology, let them feel the wrath of the people when the finally realize that they have been lied for so long, and let us marginalize them economically through the support of the people, so they do not have to persecute us or try ask us to explain, but that they must do so to the people. Let us infiltrate upon their lines, and cause their economy (and that of all their tentacles anywhere within society) and the economic system proposed by them to collapse, to awaken the people, and bring our solution, one which is final and truly alternative, spiritual, and based upon reasons and practicality, let us do so, as much as possible, without really affecting the lives of the people, but making it in such a way that all such collapse and revolution leading to the alternative with is subtle in its abruptness, and is as smooth as the change or direction of the current of the river. Our enemies will see the collapse of their systems without them expecting it, and the people will, through such trauma, grow so quick into effervescence that they will ambush our enemies from all fronts, leaving the people and them, with no option but to follow the economic system presented by us through our front groups and to follow the adherent spiritual ideologies which are subtlety presented in conjunction with this system. Bringing, ultimately, division as the problem to our enemy, and bringing our unifying solution as the only feasible, one alternative, which may even be presented by our enemies through their own will after their rendition.

Let us practice these systems and endeavors in our testing camps through any of our centers or places in which we may possess land. Let us experiment with these new systems on a small scale, and let us, through our experts in such arts, practice how we may extrapolate this to the bigger scale and whole society in which we may want to implement it to help the people. Let us always make sure that such a system works as it should in such micro-economic groups, and that it can progressively be brought to greater and greater lands and societies to work, or to modify it according to the lands and nations and the number of people within the same. Let us become experts in such arts, and modify, update or change such economic systems accordingly, always providing what is best for the spiritual and economic empowerment of the people, and, if so, is necessary for the destruction of the evil plans of our enemies. Let us plan it secretly, let us utilize small lands or islands, or any other of such means, secret or open, on land, water or air, by which we may practice such an economic system. Let us have the support of the people if such is needed when system is to implemented, and when such is not given to us, we may present other system which may be more in accordance with their society according to our experimentations, but let these experiments be executed by us, but never let its implementation be done by us, but solely by our front-groups, who will be prepared to bear with the faults and inculpations given the imperfection of society whenever they may be presented, and who will secretly be given our support with our agents. Let us, if they may not accept it, let them decide, and let them see that their proposal to continue in accordance with the plans of our enemies is faulty and inefficient, and will once again be led to follow our ways. Let us be guide by such innovative ideas and economists, and let us utilize this same experiments for the analysis of the methods by which each of these systems may further help institute our centers beyond the ups and downs of the material world and accomplish our ends of helping the people to reach their perfect state of communion with the All, and hence, with us, for we are the sole representative of the same in society, and hence to us they are left to no option but to listen and support in all of such instances and changes for the awakening and economic empowerment of all, by which we may be led that of our own. For us so we give, so we shall receive, and as good and genuine are our intentions towards the most marginalized, so we will receive the same. Let us always, in conclusion, seek to go to the cheap, the natural and to not base our existence upon the economy, but to base this upon our ideologies, ergo, God. Let us evolve through all ups and downs, and to never limit ourselves in the legal robbery of taxes as perfected by our enemies, or of usurping and appropriating resources, money and land through irrationality and immorality, but let us always seek the help of God for such manners, and to seek that through are universal presence and never-ending wisdom and goodness, one door may open if the other is closed, that one person may provided is the other deny us, and that we may found another place, resource or way if the other is not found within such place, for the possibilities are infinite, and with God by our side, contrary to our enemies, everything will be added unto us, including the economic and material question.

- As a united group, we recognize the intricate connection between political and economic dynamics, acknowledging the profound impact of economic structures on society. Our collective vision emphasizes a departure from materialistic principles, advocating for the construction of a society firmly rooted in spiritual ideals. We aim to extend our movement beyond mere economic necessity, emphasizing experimentation with alternative economic models in testing camps.

- We embark on a strategic journey, weaving our ideals into practical and stable economic systems that minimize reliance on money. Infiltrating opposing ideologies, we subtly implement change, striving to establish a society thriving on eternal principles rather than artificial economic prospects. Our collective mission centers on creating economic systems aligned with our overarching spiritual and ideological framework.

- As a united force, we envision ourselves as catalysts for societal evolution, with economic systems serving as instruments for higher spiritual and societal progress. Our approach involves continuous experimentation, analysis, and adaptation of economic systems to meet our evolving societal needs. We prioritize flexibility and adaptability in economic experimentation, always in harmony with the broader spiritual context.

- Our collective goal is to move beyond economic dependence, placing a strong emphasis on spiritual ideals as the driving force behind societal progress. We propose creating economic systems that stand as practical alternatives to prevailing ideologies, gradually gaining support through strategic implementation. As a united group, we remain committed to maintaining flexibility and adaptability in economic experimentation, always in harmony with evolving societal needs within the broader spiritual context.

9. Militia, intel agencies and warfare; deception

War, a cosmic clash of good versus evil, compels self-defense against prevailing ignorance | Rooted in the psychic and spiritual, modern warfare extends to digital realms | Emphasize timeless principles like deception | Victory hinges on aligning with universal laws and recognizing the cycle of power, knowledge, and will | Spiritual strength prevails, securing victory through unity with All | The challenge is the lack of will to eliminate evil—emphasize awakening will, knowledge, and unity | Seek unity in good, covertly uniting and strategically dividing evil | Focus on peace, fostering tranquility, and strategically funding wars for enemies' destruction | Truth counters deception; dispel ignorance, provide enlightenment, and employ unknown means to attack enemies | The greatest power lies in the spiritual realm; seek union with all | From union arises perfection, destroying imperfection, guiding us to make humanity perfect | Apply principles from ancient and modern treatises, guided by experts, paramount for our movement's survival and a tranquil, spiritual life

The dhama and self-defense chapter has left us with many doubts regarding our ways in the art of warfare. Warfare is essential to us, for the very birth of our movement has been anticipated in war, the war of good versus evil, there is no other war but his war for us. Any other war, among races, nations and religions, is nothing but a method of our enemies and their God to confront people one with the other, destroy them and more easily establish their new goals and agendas. In this sense, no war exists as a true expression of confrontation between nations, but all war is covertly directed by them towards means, or, such wars may truly exist within such an unevolved as the human one is, but it is quickly utilized by our enemies for their own purposes. The only war, thus, is good vs evil, or of us vs our enemies, or of people vs ignorance, and so on, each with their own peculiarities, but all having in common but on thing, they go back in their origination to the question of good and evil, of knowledge and ignorance. All conflict resides but in our mind, all conflict stems directly from our thoughts, beliefs and emotions, and nowhere else do we find conflict but in such psychic spheres. Therefore, all conflict, whatever its origination may be, whatever its purpose may be, has but one fundamental factor by which it acts and is manifested, and which it may be equally destroyed: the psychic paradigms and cycles of human life, and, in collective scale, of human society. If war is of tremendous importance to the continuance of our society, and all war, as so Sun Tzu is said, is based on deception, we shall, by this same manner, focus all our energies, and base our solution to this question of the aforementioned deception, and the means by which it can be prevented from its psychic cause, and that people and us do not have to suffer its indolences after its too late to diminish it. We do not like war, we do not like conflict or destruction, but we have no other options given the nature of our enemies, given the ignorance and evil, causers of such war, found within the current human society. Our incurrence into war is nothing but an incurrence in self-defense, a self-defense which is more than justified given that we stand in the positive side of the dilemma, given that we are in favor of dharma, we are the ones more aligned with the universal truth, and hence, are the ones with the greatest responsibility to direct such war at a good finalization. Being moral, natural and spiritual is not enough, we cannot live in such circumstances, and probably nowhere in the universe, by such alignment with the truth, and not have means to defend ourselves against those who oppose it, for wherever there is good there will evil around tomorrow, just as wherever is daylight today tomorrow will permeated by the shadows of dark knight. We cannot live in ignorance of evil, we have to recognize it, and we have to defend ourselves against it, for we have much forgiveness to provide to them, yet they do not offer a minuscule fraction of the same to us. Just as we try to end all evil, they try to end all good, and such warfare necessitates fighting by our part, or it necessitates the means by which its precipitation is ended before it even begins. In such a scenario, we have to possess greater warfare power, tactics and strategists than our enemies, we are to possess all means and ends by which such war is to be terminated with the smallest number of casualties and by which our ends in its unfoldment are precipitated and those of our enemies are executed. For this we have to find millinery principles and philosophies by which we may become experts at warfare. If war is the conflict by which one side subdues the will of the other, let us have such will without conflict at all, but by the destruction of our enemies given their own craziness and aberration. Let us take into account that this war is not merely physical or technological, but that its core is human psychic and very spirit given the age we live at, and that it may also be cybernetic or digital. Such modern warfare has taken new modes and channels of expressions, but the principles of war are always the same, throughout time, space and person. Hence, whatever it *modus operandi*, whatever it means of expression, we are to always focus on such universal principles of warfare, for we know that that circumstances and environment in which such war take place are relative and always-changing, we know that as circumstances move on, and the tactics of our enemies change, we will have to adapt to them, but it would be an error to be much distracted in excess about transitional relativities, for as they are relative, they are are based on deception, and hence a more clear path by which we may be further destroyed in war, for in such deception all war is based. For this very reason, we shall not operate in distraction and constant obsession with evil and her relativities into the art of deception, for in such way we are led into their means in war, but we should focus in such and such universal laws of war, as that of deception, which are maintained through time, and are guaranteed to bring success to our wars given their truthful, or eternal nature. Just as in physics and astrophysics, only that which remains is lawful, and is perfect and aligned with the Laws of All, for this very reason they are a law, and the perfect always subdues the imperfect, and the law, of cosmic origin, always subdues those who interfere with the same. You cannot escape logic, you cannot escape nature, the plant that does not follow the laws of Creation dries out and dies, in the same manner, the person that does not aligned with all intentionality with its utmost cosmic purpose, and plans out its side of polarity in the right manner, is destined to fail, and to be subdued by that side which has attained the truth, the logic found within the All, or which has become one with this same all beyond any of such laws. For how can that, which cannot be perfect, (evil), destroy or subdue the will of the eternal cosmic and universal perfection (supreme benevolence and fairness), if such is the case, and all war is based on psychic and spiritual principles as everything else is, and the stance of war is given the perfection attained in whatever sphere it may be, and such perfection is only truly attained through spiritual means which are in the positive side, why would (the awakened positive people) we be scared of our enemies, given that there is no logical way by which they may destruct us if we act according to the eternal principles of warfare, and we attain perfection in the psychic, spiritual and subliminal arenas in which such war is developed? We decipher, from such perspective and after such analysis, that war is not the means to subdue will, for such will is already subdued given the hierarchies found within the All, but that war is actually based on will as it means, and the only thing needed, for one level in the hierarchy of the all to subdue its lower arenas is will, or, if seen from a cosmic unconscious perspective, the lack of the same. That all battles are predestined from its conception, and that the only thing that determines its outcomes is the will of the benevolent part, or, the part by which the cosmic reason has been given; the perfect one. If all war and conflict is a question of will, and will stems from the mind, all war must for the same logic be mental, and if such mentality stems as a fragment of the All, of the universal mind, all war is nothing but an illusion within the free will of the all and her oblivion of the same, or, clash of the dualities and components of the composition. We need, therefore, will, will to unify with that which possesses no will; Creation. If evil is another word for division, and deception is based on division, and war is based on deception, and deception is based on knowledge, and knowledge is based on unwillingness, and such supreme will is only find in perfection, we see that one aspect leads to other, one after upon the other, and our battle always, give such universal principles, leads us to spirituality. How can the components, in their imperfect will, be of greater strength and power than the invariable supreme will, which given its perfection and hence power, is almost as if it was lacking will, how can the destruction of limbs lead to the destruction of our soul, how can the destruction of a tree lead to the destruction of nature? How can the matter be victorious over the spiritual, how can division be victorious over union, if there is no true possibility of separation, how the same be brought about in regards of of deception, if the truth is everything and every thing, how can war gain the upperhand against peace, if peace is actually found everywhere, and destruction is nothing but renewal, how can ignorance beat knowledge, if knowledge is everywhere found, even the consciousness of ignorance being knowledge, how can the unwilling beat the willing and determinant, how can the imperfect beat the imperfect, how can those in slumber, in subliminal subjugation by our enemies, of complete evil, beat the awakened benevolence? In such analysis, we see that all battle is simply an illusion of the ignorant components within the composition, and that its results if always predetermined given the power of one side over the other, and that victory is mostly assured by the will, or lack of the same in its supreme omnipotence, of the component of greater power, which is always the All, or the one more aligned with this All. Therefore, we find that we ought to always be lead back to the origin of war or peace, which is a combination, in all instances, of power, will, and knowledge, and that, given that one side possess of this than the other, this side is to win, no matter the external factors of any other circumstances external to the same. But if we analyze closely in greater clarity, we deduce that the end point root factors are solely will, for both knowledge and power are stem from the same, the former being deriving from the will to unite, to be limitless, and the latter deriving from the will of knowing everything, being that the object and the subject have become one in such previous union. We see, therefore, that all power (within the realms of microcosmic conflict operating under free will) is nothing but a willingness to unite with All, and that all lack of the same is induced by the limitations generated in the mind itself to not see beyond such ignorance. In summary, we see that all power is based on what seems to be the goal of spirituality, uniting with all, and hence all power is spiritual and mental, and all determination of the same in war, given freedom to the same, is derived from will. Thus, we see a cycle of power, knowledge and will, and the power and knowledge lead to will, and that will lead to power and knowledge. Let us have, for these reasons, **possess nothing** but a great abundance of these factors, especially that of will, for as soon as we possess will, everything else shall be added unto us, including knowledge, power, and finally the truth, which is nothing but universal power and knowledge. The only reason evil still has the upperhand on this planet is because there is a lack of will by good to eliminate it, there is a lack of will in the people to knowledge and union, which leads to more lack of will; fear and down the road on these negative factors. This always leads us to our first chapter of knowledge and good, and the transmutations of the same, it truly is the keys to our enterprises and goals. We see that our enemies know such truth, and have taken all knowledge and will to unite with All from the minds of people, for in such will all power is found, and only through such will may people awaken enough power to destroy the perfect evil. Evil on this planet is always willing and "perfect", where is such perfection and willingness on the good side, if it ever truly exists? Therefore, we must do always within our means to find ways into the will, power and knowledge, and with the combination of all these attains perfection to such a degree that we may destroy the imperfection of our enemies and of society, let us to be guided by these principles in regards to warfare:

Division; hate and fear, beget evil, we shall seek unity, seek union in good always united covertly and through all means without people or our enemies noticing, seek division in evil, divide wherever it is united, and that such division leads to the union with good.

Evil leads to war, we shall always seek peace. We shall seek peace in the people, we shall find means to end their conflicts, we shall fund wars in our enemies, and that such war always leads to peace by their own destruction, we shall take advantage of their internal conflicts for our benefit, or we shall initiate given their own trap of malevolent tones.

War is on deception, we shall always seek the truth. We shall bring the truth to the people and awaken their consciousness, and deception to our enemy, in order to bring to truth, we shall attack through all kinds of means unknown and operating under masks of all kinds.

Deception is based on ignorance, we shall always seek knowledge. We shall provide knowledge of all kinds to people, we shall provide ignorance to our enemy, given that such ignorance leads to knowledge by which their actions are terminated. The greatest attack is the one whose origin and operation is unknown, let us attack our enemies.

Power stems from the will for all previous factors in their positive counterpart, we seek will and determination. We give will, aspirations and determination to the people, hope for the betterment of humanity, we subdue and eliminate the will of our enemies, we escape from their will and transmute it towards our goals.

The greatest power is the spiritual one, given that we become one with the All, we seek to unite with all in consciousness. We provide means to the people to unite with the All, and to open their mind to new realities. We reduce the minds and consciousness of our enemies, and transmutate their expansive aspirations towards the positive side.

From such union with all and natural role in our essence, we arrive at perfection and we destroy all that is imperfect given the negative counterparts of all previous factors. We ought to make humanity and people perfect in all degrees, we ought to destroy the so-called perfection of our enemies.

- And in general, to apply these principles in their many variations as explained in the warfare and spiritual treatises of ancient and modern times, all of which are always based on universal principles, and let us know this and much more on war, and be guided by the greatest of experts on this art, for it is of much importance for our survival as a movement. For this knowledge may be the one leading to greatest rewards, and for a more tranquil and spiritual life free from the torments of our enemies.

- In delving into the intricacies of warfare and our movement's stance, it becomes apparent that war is not merely a physical conflict but a manifestation of the eternal battle between good and evil. While wars among nations may seem diverse, they are tools manipulated by enemies to exploit the innate human dichotomy of good versus evil, knowledge versus ignorance. Our movement, rooted in the principles of dharma and self-defense, views war as an act of necessity, justified by our alignment with universal truth and our responsibility to guide conflicts toward positive resolutions.

- A critical realization emerges that the core of war extends beyond the physical, delving into the realms of the psychic and spiritual. Modern warfare, with its varied expressions, necessitates a focus on timeless, universal principles such as deception, rooted in their eternal and truthful nature. Amid the ever-changing circumstances, the importance lies in adhering to these fundamental laws rather than getting entangled in transitional relativities.

- The analysis further explores the cosmic and spiritual dimensions of war, emphasizing that battles are illusions within the cosmic mind's free will. The narrative underscores the intrinsic subjugation of will within cosmic hierarchies, emphasizing the need for aligning with Creation to counteract the divisive nature of evil. The cyclical relationship between power, knowledge, and will emerges as a guiding principle, advocating for an abundance of these factors for ultimate success in war.

- In providing principles for warfare, the focus turns to unity, seeking peace amid conflict, and the unveiling of truths while fostering ignorance in enemies. The spiritual dimension takes precedence, urging alignment with the cosmic All for the attainment of perfection and the annihilation of imperfections. The imperative lies in exploring knowledge, will, and power to guide humanity toward perfection, countering the prevailing forces of evil.

10. The extraterrestrial question

The illogical of denying extraterrestrial existence | Egocentrism blinds humanity| Enemies deceive, distorting science for their agenda. | Their link to negative entities transcends worlds | Some humans are not entirely human, tied to ancient extraterrestrial origins | To change the alien panorama, shift knowledge, consciousness and intellect to perceive new realities | Earth is a zombified farm, negative and positive entities coexist | To perceive the extra we are to change the intra | Reveal truth | Study as no one else | Defends our agents and people from the evil entities| Infiltrate evil mystery societies | Preserve evidence and prophesize the future| Contactees' knowledge further boosts our power | Collaborate with positive aliens for change| Study undiscovered races, learn from them for mutual victory and awakening.

It seems to me, and to reason itself, that it is an illogical idea to think that we are alone in this universe. There are millions of animals upon this planet, what makes us think that there are not equally millions of such species out there? What makes us think, in this egocentric side we so much indulge in, that we are the only so-called intelligent race upon this universe? This is one of the greatest phallacies which have recently overtaken the human social mind. Our enemies are well-versed in the Art of Deception, and they have created a reality which was constructed solely to deceive society, and they have distorted all science and knowledge to benefit their agenda and that agenda of the demons they worship and collaborate with... We know that this agenda of our enemies is, therefore, intimately linked with such negative entities of other worlds and dimensions. We know that many of our enemies are either hosts of these non-human entities or they are themselves not human at all. The foundation of their entitlement is found within their extraterrestrial, "Godly, divine" origin. We know, as part of our secret knowledge, which is not so secret as unknown, that many of a great part of the races of human within this planet, are a not 100% human if not at all, and that many of the pyramids, edifices and other monuments of such kind are a remembrance and testimony of the passage of these ancestors of these in this planet. For, if we look closely into such proofs, of historical, anthropological, and biological and linguistic science we will surely reach the conclusion that alien beings are in existence, and that they have come to this planet in the past. This problem is solely a problem of knowledge, of consciousness, and somewhat, of intellect. For the knowledge is being hidden by our enemies from the public so they do not ever find out that many of their companions are being abducted and abused by these entities as they abuse the other entities who inhabit this planet, and that many of Earth manuscripts and scriptures speak on these, yet they are hidden in our enemies libraries. For the consciousness is being held hostage and shrinked in excess by our enemies, so the people cannot even perceive within their radius of visualization, and so they cannot perceive beyond their cultural programming, and perception, which is equally kept crude and materialistic by any of such mundane pastimes and so-called obligations they are covertly obliged to do. And lastly, for the intellect is being and suppressed in the academic institutions, and reason is being applied partially, and only in a empirical and materialistic sense, which auto-imposes upon the alumni, notions of limitations and lack of questioning of reality, instead provided and embodied in indoctrination and excess assumption and acceptance of what has already been given by their superiors. Thus, we see that the extra-terrestrial question is not so much "extra", meaning, of the outside world, but actually, INTRA, inside our minds, inside the perception of each and every human, for as inside so outside. To change society we therefore, have to change their inside vibration and perception, and in such a manner we may start to open their perception to new realities and dimensions, and hence to possibility of existence of these entities, especially those of a positive demarcation, and ultimately their possible future contact with these. In this same intrinsic character, we find precisely what distinguishes us from them, that is, our knowledge, our consciousness and our intellect, and we have, through a final analysis of the whole situation, change nothing but their perception to the same level to which ours is differential to theirs. For it is not enough that only we (a minority against billions) know of such existence, this is in now way enough for these entities to contact us publicly too, these entities visiting solely do so in cooperation with our enemies, and for the only purpose of utilizing humanity as a farm, not as companion in the same grade, this is what is done to the masses in slumber. But if we, through our capacities to overturn these vibrations, establish in them a greater consciousness, they will finally come to realize the truth, and our contact with these positive entities, instead of the negative ones, will be able to be brought about in a mass scale throughout human society, and our enemies will have not option but to putrefy in their cooperation with the negative entities, to who they so much ritual and sacrifice destine, and which is being passed from generation to generation, in this extra-culture of which they much knowledge possess and therein indulge, refrain to open it from its secret state to the masses, these so-called mystery religions are nothing but the same means by which they, and these negative entities, seek to covertly establish an malevolent empire in this planet. In conclusion, Earth is but a farm zombified planet, in which negative and positive live in all ramifications of the ground (intraterrestrial species are reminiscences from the ancient times of Atlantis and Lemuria), air and water, the former taking advantage of the current state of slumber and of Kali Yuga, while covertly and secretly collaborating with our enemies in the elites for the same total consummation of this state in a much greater degree and upon the whole Earth, the latter, only watching and restricting the over-abuse created by these formers, and communicating with positive, indigenous and awakened people, equally privately and in secret, as they have the principle of non-interference, from time to time. In the end, we see, that the question, as it was mentioned in one our first protocol (which was inspired by one of our positive extraterrestrial companions), is always one of knowledge and ignorance, of good vs evil, and for all these we shall effectuate the following protocols in relation to any of such extraterrestrial entities:

- We shall find ways by which the truth of their existence is to be revealed to the people, we shall fund societies, front-groups and movements which are consecrated with the intent of studying such beings and having contact with them through all kinds of practices, spiritual or otherwise, we shall our student know from a young of their existence and think critically and rationally in such terms, and we shall utilize any of such agents to speak and express much of such truths in all kinds of media and channels of expression.
- We shall ourselves, in conjunction with our agents, study deeply such knowledge, and let it be of such degree and discernment through our superior intellectual and spiritual capacity, that we render clearly the truth from the untrue, and the distorted from the unadulterated, given the many tricks of the

same channel used by our enemies and negative races, so that we may not be indulgent in any false dissidence utilized by our counterparts.

- Given these two previous points, we shall equally provide are agents and those in contact and in study to such entities, be provided with knowledge and means of the spiritual kind and others, by which they can combat and defend from any of such entities of the negative order, and methods by which they can perceive and identify their evil from their benevolent, and their truth from their illusion; proceeding their activation of consciousness following our precepts.
- Let us, subsequent to the previous point, find ways by which we may find the origin of such attacks or the derivations of such negative expressions, let us, with the help of these previously mentioned and other of our agents, especially prepared by us, infiltrate in such evil and mysterious societies which contact these races for evil means and ends, and let us destroy them from the inside and we have so commented on the transmutation chapter.
- Let us, in conjunction with the means described the history and prophecy chapters, prescribe these same means for the persecution of all kind of physical evidence and artifacts regarding the existence of such entities, and let us well think if it shall be revealed to the public or not, and to what extends it may benefit us in any of our missions, in spiritual or technological aspects especially.
- Given this previous point, let us find contactees or start-seeds or infiltrate in their societies where we may gather more information ingrained within their mind in relation to their past lives, and particular powers of physical, intellectual and spiritual kind by which they may help us accomplish our means, and by which we may further bring to light the extraterrestrial reality and combat their evil side.
- A *posteriori* to the previous point, let them conduct us to the places and means by which we may further contact our positive alien companions, and means by which we may collaborate, at least through interchange of knowledge and *bene placito*, for the consummation of our objects and their hopes regarding the change of Earth from what state to the other, provided it is better for us, in decency and spiritual vibration to them.
- Let us not only gather knowledge of such artifacts as mentioned in the previous points, but let us deeply, study, and go as far as to create new sciences in relation to ufology, exology, and crypto-zoology, in relation to these races, let us clearly study their places of habitation, the many races different to humanity which exist underground and underwater, let us contact them, collaborate to reach the ends of both parties regarding our evil counterparts and let us use this same knowledge to find these uncommon or not yet discovered races, intelligent or developing, within this planet.

- Finally, given all these previous points; our study of the extra and intraterrestrial races, find ways by which we can learn much from them, of their genes and process of intermarriage or genetic sciences and technologies, so we may build such new forms of life and technologies, so that we through this same technology and spiritual knowledge, help them be victorious to the enemies and us over our enemies, rendering through this cooperation both victorious, and finding means by which the truth of their existence and good intentions towards the whole of humanity may be further given to all the people on Earth, proceeding the awakening process of which they so much shall inspire and offer support, especially through us and many of these other people in contact with them.

- The notion that we are alone in the universe is deemed illogical, given the multitude of species on Earth. Despite our egocentrism, there's a blindness to the potential existence of other intelligent races. Deception by enemies distorts science to serve their agenda, linking them to negative entities beyond our world. Some humans, part of races on Earth, have extraterrestrial origins, evident in historical monuments.

- To reshape society, a shift in consciousness and intellect is crucial to perceive new realities. Earth is described as a zombified farm, where negative and positive entities coexist. The extraterrestrial question is seen as an internal challenge within our minds.

- The outlined protocols aim to address this challenge: revealing the truth about extraterrestrial existence, studying deeply, defending against negative entities, infiltrating societies collaborating with them, preserving evidence responsibly, gaining knowledge from contactees, and collaborating with positive extraterrestrial entities. The goal is to learn from undiscovered races, contributing to mutual victory and the awakening of humanity.

- This multifaceted approach involves scientific study, spiritual development, and collaboration with positive entities to bring about a positive change, challenging the hidden agendas of negative forces.

11. Society, visibility, labeling and legality

Oppose infra-human status, defy irrationality | Strategically awaken masses, face intentional enemies | Battle societal imperfections, counter externalized ignorance | Protocols awaken, counter animality | Operate above norms, secrecy counters prejudice | Masks influence covertly, prejudice on messenger destroyed by invisibility, strategic communication | Covert operation with tricks, public-private distinct, hidden agents | Present truth deceptively, combat societal illusion through the same | Revive means, adapt to external pressures, truth universally | Operate beyond labels, embrace absolute morality | Proud of illegality, self-defense against injustice, defend morally | Defend against enemies, moral and illegal means combined | Expose immoral acts covertly, challenge societal irrationality | Legitimize self-defense immorally, face unjust attacks | Challenge irrational laws, immoral acts against the people | Superior morality justifies, operate beyond legal constraints | Utilize dissenting ideas, illegal yet moral acts counter unfair treatment | Embrace diverse protocols, technological, spiritual, psychological | Immorality justified, self-defense against societal prejudices and injustices.

Human society, as it is currently functioning and established, is everything but human, rather infra-human, denoting only qualities aberrant, or contrary to reason, nature and truth. People in a state of slumber cannot be dealt with such aforementioned pretenses, but only through the contrary artificiality and counterparts of such aforementioned qualities provided by our enemies. How are we to relate in a sociological aspect with such people and our enemies? Given that these two are opposed to us, one intentionally and with all premeditation, the other unconsciously, with all ignorance and minute consciousness. One, which possesses knowledge but is evil, the other being just as ignorant of this same knowledge yet benevolent if knowledgeable and open to expand their consciousness. Therefore, this question of us in relation to these groups of society, and these subsequent questions of knowledge and morality in relation to us and our ideology, and modus of thinking and their is to be taken with much care, for in it rests the continuance of our society within such an ignorant, unconscious and marginalizing society, full of dogma and all such imperfections which provided by our enemies, lead to their own destruction, and conjunction, to the destruction of us, and all that is good by the overt guidance of our enemies. Therefore, the social aspect of such protocols is summarized in waking people up, while keeping at keeping their externalization of ignorance, unconsciousness and animality, and in keeping these same latter aspects against our enemies in their intentional form, hoping that they may be destroyed, for they are both knowledgeable and evil, therefore twice as important to destroy as those in slumber in the lower masses of society. But being this latter paradigm as aberrant as the former, given that therefrom it descends. Therefore, let us know how we may, in such social aspects, interact with these counterparts of ours so we may render these same objects of conjugating our objects and their into one, unifying the means and practices in a rational and spiritual way.

First, our entity, our organization, as a group or movement within human society must expand beyond any legal and populational aspect, or any of such limitations as desired by society and their governors (the puppets of our enemies), limitations which are led by a governmental system which leads to more and more tyranny and limitation in all aspects, while pretending to the contrary, this limitation, is sure to imposed upon us by such social and legislative means. Our means and methods shall be always above such limitations as they have been imposed upon humans in all areas of their lives. Our means to do that may be executed through all means, even if they may be seen from the outside as falling outside the Laws Of Creation, as in the chapter of self-defense, we have no other option but to recur to these methods, as those of secrecy and overt influence throughout human society. Our movement shall refer from the public whenever it is faced by backlash or prejudice by the people or the government, we shall have no other option but to infiltrate and awaken people through means of secrecy, for only through secrecy is prejudice and illogical perceptions of such kind rendered ineffective by the same ignorance on the origination of such knowlege. People are accustomed to judge people in their social aspects, not the knowledge presented itself, they do not judge according to the message but according to the messenger. If knowledge is given in hypothetical sense, to such or such person with total ignorance of their origin and ways by which its origination point may be judged, the probabilities of working and rationalizing according to such knowledge and not through the lenses of sociological prejudice are diminished and suppressed in turn of message and content rationalization, which pays attention to the contents and not to the forms. Society is much accustomed to judging according to the apparent, and not through the substantial, this and that in an irrational manner, this or that in a rational manner. Let us therefore, understand the ways by which we may be prejudiced by society, and the ways we may be understood, so we may present and employ our means and objects, overtly or covertly accordingly. Let us therefore, not expose ourselves to these irrational and negative vibrations of such ignorant sleeping beings, let ourselves be known to us and our objects, but never to be known to these which unjustly judged us, such as relatives, friends or any other of such civil people who may have in their pretenses our destruction or marginalization. Let us operate in secret, in relation to our appertaining to this group, let us communicate freely on such channels, even if public, if we are the only ones to know of our true intentions and identity. Let us utilize all kinds of tricks, masks and any of these to operate freely with all vehemence yet with all secrecy to our closest relations in the social aspect. Let us operate under all types of entities and names of different kinds so that we may be everywhere known, everywhere influencing, yet never under revealing our truth, nor our relations with each of our circles. Let us operate as if we were invisible to such promoters of prejudice, only known to ourselves and our agents, only revealing the content of the message, but never the content of its origin, so that prejudice and irrationality are never in any shape or form operated against by these mortifiers. In such a way we may reveal what is only to be intended to be known by the masses. There is no other way in such conditions, than to present the truth through deception, given the immersion in illusion as implemented by our enemies towards these people. Let us for such objects create a public identity, by which people may be content by not knowing much about but by indulging in our messages. Let our private identity be kept private and unknown to all circles, except our own. Let us hide agents and create front-groups which pretend to be our center group, to work in all openness, given that such prejudice may be directed against them, but that we may maintain ourselves occult to never die under any of such circumstances. Never let anyone outside our circle, nor any of these agents of our enemies which pretend to be our friends, know our true identity nor true nature and objects. Let us always provide false identities, means and objects, so that we may not be attacked irrationally when such is the case, let us have the justification because of this same marginalization to deceive people of such facts of meaningless nature, but to never lie to them regarding that which matters, the Laws of Creation and the infinite power of the spirit inside each man and woman. Let our movement grow beyond any of such labels imposed upon us by society, let our movement grow as nature itself, that whenever one plant is destroyed by fire in some place on Earth, she may plant herself somewhere else through rain. That whenever any of such infortunes or means happen to be obfuscated by such external social pressures, we may revive this same means and brothers of ours somewhere else, in another time, and in other circumstances. But never let any of these methods and identities of public stance have any relation to the other, so that our influence extends beyond their short and minute perception, which is solely subjected to prejudice at all times. Let the truth be presented by itself, for in such absolute and universal manner it inherits the greatest of powers, as messenger who leaves his letter at the door of the people in slumber, but of whom the identity is unknown to the recipient, but only to the sender of the messenger. Let too, this message be presented in the most natural manners, as if it was a deception by our enemies, for these people in slumber will only believe, by their mental and cultural programming, what has been said by our enemies. Let this sender, therefore, be infiltrated in the same senders operated by our enemies, through all kinds of written and audiovisual means, digital, verbal or of any other channel of expression. Provided this, the label is going to imposed not at us but at our enemies, the prejudice which has so many times been directed against us will be directed at our enemies, and this ignorance will be transmuted into further knowledge, a knowledge provided by us of the senders of the senders, of the content of the messenger, which are unknown to the people. Let us present the truth of their comportment and the reality which has been hidden to the people regarding their evil, then, if people do not wake to such aberrant acts, it may mean that they are to be considered equally evil, and hence, our enemies. If people are presented with the truth, and they do not wake up, it is because they do not want to, and they continue to be well comforted in such ignorance, hence, making them equally our enemies, or making them of such intellect and consciousness as to not be considered worth the struggle. Let us, in such ends previously explained, change our means, and operate under any of these variances whenever possible, of identity, visibility, and labeling. Leading, in such contrivances, solely to a question of knowledge or ignorance, rationality or irrationality, and of the dilemma of presenting the same given these opposite messengers and messages.

Let us, when such a dilemma, directly concerns our relation with our enemy, operate under many different names and orders by which we may counteract their illogical legislations of irrational order. For these legislations, and their legislators, judiciaries and executors, are not to be taken as truth or just as long as they are irrational or against the Laws of Creation, but solely based upon the irrational or aberrant laws of men, precisely against nature and morale. For a crime is not a sin, for the relative not absolute, for the illogical cannot be fair, nor can the illogical be unfair. For the government, and those behind it, have no right to subdue the people to their will of the jurisdictions of their laws as long as these are illogical and opposed to those of Creation, and as long as this same government indulges in that which they so much unjustly persecute. For the government (ergo our enemies) persecute the stealers, yet they are the first one to steal through taxes, for the government persecutes the killers, yet the create legislations which indirectly kill people through theater confrontation, for the government persecutes those who insult and protest, sometimes against this same enemies of our, yet they are the first to do this same act and oppress the liberties and natural right of the people, for the government persecute the rapists, yet they are the first ones to violate us, not only physically, but mentally and spiritually, and so on with any of these immoral and unnatural acts. Yet they do it in such a manner that they may be labeled as moral and fair through covert means and secrecy. What right and moral, therefore, do they have to effectuate such injustices against the people if they do it merely through rude force, as so would an animal which seeks to kill its prey? Don't we, therefore, have the right to defend ourselves? For we do not need to change what is already perfect and fair, but what is imperfect and unfair, isn't such modus operandi unfair and deserving of an equal attack as a way of defense by our part? Is there anything more evil and deserving of damnation and condemnation than pretending to be moral and imposing such morality, when in reality you are the most immoral and the greater dictator of evil? Thus, we, by incurring secrecy and so-called illegal activities, are not actually evil as so portrayed by our enemies to the masses, but simply the seekers and demonstrator of the utmost truth, one which falls outside the demarcation and irrational laws of our enemies. Let us confide ourselves in secrecy to these moral yet illegal acts, while exposing through covert and overt means their immoral yet legal acts, so that people may wake to the truth beyond any of such limitations imposed by the government and our enemies behind. In such cases we have the right to defend ourselves through immorality, for the immoral is not defending yourself against those who so pretend to be, rather it is them, that through their attack to the innocent and sleeping people, are the most immoral among the immoral. In no way can the moral be deemed as illegal, for those who so say are themselves immoral, and in no way, can equally the immoral be imposed as legal, as they so do, for legislations are nothing but the manifestation of relativity and immorality as long as they, and hence, unauthorized through logic and the laws of creation, which are those of Nature. By such same means which they use, and such illogical justifications, we may present to them the fair and logical counterpart. That we are entitled to operate as we like and to operate such and any of these illegal acts in secret, as long as they are moral, and that, if we are presented with reprimand by these same impostors of the inversion, we have the right to be immoral given their immorality. That, as they so use force, we have the superior right and power, given our superior morality; by this doctrine of superior morality and consciousness of the truth we have the right to be immoral against them and to defend ourselves from their attacks. Let us, therefore, be illegal and let us be proud of such illegality, as long as it is not within the relative morality, but within the absolute one provided and found within ourselves and Nature. Let us, just as so precise before, have no label in the legal aspect, but to be labeled only under the absolute label of morality, let us everywhere operate through these dissenting ideas and illegal yet moral acts, and let us utilize or means to counter these same previously spoken of unfair treatment by our state and the enemy, which is contrary and so much in persecution by our Luciferian enemies, who practices the inversion of such order, and deceive the people to believe wrong and be deceived through all manners, methods and means possible. Ultimately, let use any of these herein explained protocols, such as the technological, the spiritual or the psychological, let us be immoral only when in self defense, we may need to fight any of such prejudices, ignorance, dogmas and injustices, as direct against us by the people, who lack our consciousness, and are putrid by the evil rained down by our enemies, to which we shall have not mercy as the causers of such collective hypnosis and indulgence in the aberrant points by which humanity has lost its face.

- "Human society, as it currently functions, is infra-human, denoting qualities aberrant to reason, nature, and truth. Interaction with slumbering individuals requires countering artificiality and counterparts imposed by enemies. Societal protocols focus on awakening people, maintaining externalization of ignorance, and countering intentional and unintentional opposition. The organization must expand beyond legal and societal limitations, operating above imposed restrictions. Secrecy is key to minimizing prejudice; public identity is created to influence, but private identity remains unknown. Truth is presented through deception to overcome societal illusions. In social aspects, changing means and operating under various identities unifies rational and spiritual practices."

- "In the sociological realm, the entity navigates irrational legislation, avoiding prejudice, and influencing through secrecy. The movement uses tricks and masks to operate covertly, ensuring rational and spiritual practices prevail. Public identity masks the private truth, preserving the essence of the message regardless of societal prejudice. The organization operates beyond societal labels, growing organically like nature. Publicly, the truth is presented through various channels, exposing irrational legislation and influencing people's perceptions. The dilemma involves presenting the truth through deception to counteract enemies' manipulations."

- "Societal relations involve operating under different names and orders, countering illogical legislation, and defending against enemies' injustices. Secrecy and 'illegal' activities are embraced to protect against immoral attacks by enemies. The organization defends itself through morality against the immorality of enemies. Operating illegally becomes a means of self-defense, justified by the superior morality of the organization. The focus is on being labeled under absolute morality, not relative legalities, and using dissenting ideas and illegal yet moral acts to counter unfair treatment by the state and enemies."

- "In conclusion, the entity employs multifaceted protocols, including technological, spiritual, and psychological, to counteract societal hypnosis and injustices. The goal is to awaken humanity from collective hypnosis induced by Luciferian enemies, fighting prejudices, ignorance, dogmas, and societal injustices with unwavering determination."

12. The Earthly Mother; Shakti, supports our cause

Nature is the only header | Society's imbalance correctable through natural acts | Aberration causes physical, mental, spiritual diseases | Return through nature's wisdom | Earth's consciousness reacts to human sins, awakening imminent | Conscious cooperation with Earth's forces essential | Feminine energy rational and reactive | Mass purification through 4 elements | Awakened ones cooperate as Earth's militia, fighting aberrant people | Promote nature-friendly ideologies, centers, movements | Instill love for nature in children | Trained botanical experts use nature's remedies as response to trauma, leading to targeted awakening | Experts in mineralogy, chemistry, physics create unbeatable, eco-friendly technologies | Apply principles for animal welfare, minimize suffering | Hack and destroy systems promoting cruelty | Raise awareness against immorality | Awakening linked to spiritual and neo-humanist principles, society's change crucial | Help animals for societal awakening, nature reciprocates | Victory leads to the rule of truth and justice against disruptors of dharma.

There is no greater reminder of the truth than Mother Nature; Parecelsus has said: "no one heals a sick human but nature". In this same sense, the sickness within the mentality and spirituality of the majority if not almost all of human society can in no way be brought back to a state of balance than through the acts of Nature. It is in, our daily sains against nature, as Hippocrates said, that we bring ourselves in the damnation of disease, be it physical, mental or spiritual, and there is no way from escaping such aberrant mode of life so common now in society, than through the knowledge of nature. That by their own will, human beings may choose to return to their natural state, their state of righteousness, their state align with their inherent qualities within the All; dharma. But, given the reticence, or even worse, ignorance, by the part of humans, of their deviation from such natural Laws and Nature herself, they will have to suffer the utmost abrupt consequences by which the truth will be presented to them in a matter of nothingness, in a very short period of time. If one looks back into the natural events throughout history, and one studies their effect only fauna and flora, one will many notice that such changes took place before such elements of nature could even defend themselves, in some kind of traumatic experience, which is in no way more awakening than by making the victims realize their ignorance. These changes which may take place, will severely bring changes in the human psyche and consciousness; bringing humanity out of such a state of slumber in which it currently indulges. Really, this change is not only merely a spiritual change which is to be over-complicated, but a change which can be understood from a simplistic emotional outlook. Who has not realized that when humans confront the most difficult situations, is when they evolve the most, when they come face to face with the truth, it is in that moment that they start to develop spiritual aspirations. For when we realize the ephemeral and meaningless sense of our body and ego, we see that what really matters extends beyond this superficiality, which in turn manifests itself through all society by dint of our enemies' plans and means. Such downs push us to further seek the truth, to further question the nature of reality and the finality of truthfulness, nor to knock the door with fervor and genuinity to arrive at such ends. But humans, sadly, in such a state in which our enemies have engineered to establish their consciousness, dwell in all ignorance in such aberration, and lack the will, nor the conditions to arrive at such ends by asking, seeking or knocking. Therefore, how is it that we can cooperate with this natural feminine force found within Mother Earth, so that she can help to implement this new awakening in human society and reach a new state of true spirituality within planet Earth?

It serves us well to remember that this force, is a conscious force, not a blind force, not a force which reacts through crudity, but which manifests these only by the conscious effort of its intrinsic counterpart Shiva, Shakti, the female creative force, manifests itself by subordination to the ethereal masculine force which permeates the all. So, we get here, that this feminine energy, is equally masculine when it so needs to become, and that it does operate out of irrationality or accidentality, but out of reaction, a rational natural reaction to an equally aberrant action; that actions established, daily through small sins by human beings. This consciousness found within planet Earth is growing angrier and angrier each day by the habituation of humans to such aberrations through the recent millennia, but when Earth has had enough of such aberrant comportment, she will have no option but to strike back at their children, and through the scolding of its inner consciousness, guided by the cosmic powers, establish back the spiritual and righteous sense so long lost in the human minds. These forces will bring into conjunction the 4 elements, those of fire, earth, wind and water, each of those will come after the other, in such an order that human society may finally be purified, it truly is a purification process, as the one employed by any of such groups, by which the consciousness is refreshed and we are born anew. This process will be in mass scale and it will suppose not the mere change of an individual, but that of all of humanity. These events, support, for they are brought by the cosmic universal forces which we defend, hence this process to awaken people, is the same force and aspirations, in its intrigue, of our desires to awaken society and bring it to a new state. The only difference is that we see this process through the eyes of human reason and knowledge, while Mother Earth extends far beyond in consciousness and sees it with the eyes of God. Our energy is one which manifests from the micro to macro; from the few awakened and sometimes through our enemies, to the masses in slumber, while that of Mother Earth, by its macrocosmic stance, relates to human society as a microcosm which is to be adjusted within her body. Just like the works of the human body which are effectuated that specific part of the human body back to its natural state, such as the mechanisms by which body and its immune system intend to fight a pathogen, so it will Mother Earth destroy the current aberrant human society.

We, the awakened ones, which are part, in this same sense, of the militia of Mother Earth, will equally have to effectuate such awakening. This awakening is first, a conscious one, regarding the inherent aberrant state of mind of humanity, which may be changed by knowledge, wisdom, spirit and reason. But there is a second relation of humanity to Nature; nature itself, not her manifestation within human spirit and mind, body and society, but of the relation of these in the extrinsic sense to Nature. We shall fight as Nature's cooperatives, by, whenever and wherever so possible, helping grow in her natural state, and not implement any artificial means by which we may destroy her. We will create ideologies and centers and means by which this same are to be manifested, we will create in humanity a sense of love for Nature, which will take place by various fronts and all means possible. We will ourselves always choose the most nature-friendly of all options in the externalization of our consciousness in the material world and our relation with the same. We will make people realize the consequences of destroying nature and not following her Laws, we will create means by which we will artificially teach naturality, but never will we let this artificial means, by which we awaken such people, develop and occupy greater space in their minds than Nature. But humanity is guided by our enemies that we have no option but to present the benefits of nature through artificial equipment. We will instantly presume through such agents the ways in which nature is preferable to such artificial pleasures and mundanities. We should especially instill, from a young age, a sense of care for

Nature in the minds of children, so a generation can grow with such naturality within their consciousness. We will equally in this process, create trained agents which will establish movements, everywhere possible, where society can be guided towards the path of the natural, and for the care of the same. All agents, by being awarered and having such connection with Nature, will equally utilize this for our benefit, for as we take care and promulgate the natural doctrine with our agents, she will equally be responsible, as long as we follow the Laws of Creation, of helping through our ups and downs and destroying our enemies whenever such case may be needed. We will especially train these in the forces of nature which stand beyond the field of visibility of the masses, and the 5 elements will be rendered in our favor by following her Laws. Any of these following we will fervor study in a metaphysical sense by which its relation with the human spirit and mind will further enable us to control it for positive means. We will train experts of botany and zoology, who will render us free of any ailments or the same by which we may help the people, especially when this same help has failed to be provided by our enemies. We will be a natural and right alternative, and hence they will trust us and our natural ideology and nature more than the artificial tactics of our enemies. These will know of every plant, and the benefits of these to the human body, mind and spirit, and how these effects may be transmuted, diverting or focusing in different ways through positive metaphysical means. We will take care of these as no one else us, all our constructions will have natural sense given to them, they will be a bastion by which Mother Earth will further use us, and we use in a cooperation to awaken humanity. We may even utilize such plants of various kinds for other means of attack whenever they may be necessary, we may use these plants to bring different states of mind and spirit, especially when we have no other option and the situation is presented as an urgency. We will possess such botanical resources free from the artificial bureaucracy of the state, and may hide any of these when such is the case needed and whenever we may be in persecution through their evil efforts to demonize the natural for the termination of all of such ailments of body, mind and spirit. We shall create front-groups to provide for the creation of such extensive knowledge, database and means by which this natural aspect of plants is to be taken care for and whose uses may be further brought upon the innocent people. Let us especially promote and utilize agents, individually or collectively, to provide such natural remedies to the people, through physical, spiritual or digital means by which any of our other agents or partners may lend us a hand. By helping them in such a manner they will have no option but to believe in Mother Nature and take care of her. Our intentions are genuine, and by such charity to people through nature, they will provide with the same respect to nature and us. On the other hand, our enemies, which pretend to help nature through such means, will appear as frauds given the perfection and authenticity by which we are superior to them in such a sense. There is no better way to get people acquainted with nature than through the trauma of attempting to defy her, therefore, whenever possible, we will construct centers in which people seek us in such situations when all their artificial possibilities have been consumed, in we stand as the only solution to their problems, we in such moment of trauma, will, in al naturality and covertly, present to them our ancient wisdom regarding these topics, so that at the same time they feel their relieve and gratefulness, they ought to have to option but to be grateful to us and Mother Earth, a process which ends in the total awakening of person. The power and artificiality of our enemies will succumb as we provide newer and newer possibilities for a quick mass scale production of organic and natural products, and by dint of the correct and perfect use of botanics and science such as homeopathy and herbalism to heal people, this will turn the people more and more towards our solution of truthful and natural origin; due in part, to our inherent superior nature. We will use all means possible to make people aware of such superiority and construct means by which the artificial and pharmaceutical products manufactured by our enemies lack demand and so they can finally stop doing business with the health and dignity of people and plants.

We will train and possess experts in mineralogy, chemistry, physics and any other of such fields pertaining to the so-called non-living natural world, by which we may understand the deeper feeling of our Earthy Mother, and we create the greatest and most natural (therefore, perfect) of the technologies, which will manifest impossible to surpass by our enemies. We will construct and become experts on these materials, by which we will become as alchemists and change one to the other at will by the infinite power of our spirit. We will manifest such love for the very molecules of all these elements, as if they were our brothers and sisters, that these will develop a love for us, and through these positive vibrations destroy all negative frequencies emanating from the artificial weapons utilized by our enemies. Our construction process, which takes into the account the many geometries (such pyramids and any other of such kind) of nature and their capacity to provide for our spiritual aspirations, will be based on these natural non-contaminating elements, which will easily be recycle or re-utillzed, and which prove to be a strong as those utilized by our enemies. We will develop these intricacies from the least conceived places, and we shall possess the least known, yet geniuses regarding such topics. Stones and crystal will equally be utilized as spiritual weapons, by which we may construct such spiritual instruments whenever we may need them, let us reach such knowledge of the minerals that we utilize them to enter and manipulated the astral and spiritual fields, and let us know their composition as no one else does, so that we may render any of the enemies attacks useless. Let us equally utilize organic materials for such a construction process, and let us through a combination of the organic and inorganic, rest assured that we fulfill our natural mission, yet that it is strong enough to defend us against any of these enemies. We will equally, as we have done in regards to botanics, create font-groups, ideologies, and associations to take care of nature in relation to such inorganic elements. They will have restrictions to become nature-friendly, as they bring the best out of Mother Earth. We may effectuate such changes through means of dubious origin or legality for our enemies, but its morale and spirit goes beyond any of such illogical laws of men. Whenever our enemy disregards the law, and the damage caused is far worse than their decease, we shall use any of our secret means to convince them to change their opinions, and if such is the not the case, we shall render their means ineffective by providing them with infiltrated agents of such kind who will establish wrong methods and procedures, leading to the failure of such artificial inorganic enterprises. Let us in this superiority, be differential to our enemies and defend ourselves of our attacks through any of the other means mentioned and through the wrath and corroding systems of delusion within the people's mind.

Finally, when it comes to animal life, we shall utilize the same principles found within our spiritual practices. Let us equally be rational at all times even so, and we may find that we may have to break any of such principles given very specific situations, especially as Mother Earth so disrupts herself to remove her diseased humanity. Even in such instances, let us utilize in all possible means by which our *abanico* of possibilities may expand so that we may not have to regard these laws and practices in relation to morality. Let us treat animals, and our agents with such love that we may develop a sense of spirit in them, so that they may develop psychic propensities of subtler expression, and by this same spiritual connection and even telepathic communication with them we may utilize them for any of such things discussed. Let us protect them especially when they are unnecessarily killed and whenever their treatment is not the one which ought to be. Let us create associations for their protection and agents which may help them and train them to favor us everywhere through their various and many skills, just as plants manifest different properties. Let us always raise the voice of such injustices, through these front-groups and movements, let us especially do it through progressive and subtle means, when the mentality of the person is found to be in reticence to such ideals, and let us make abrupt whenever we found fervor in such individual. Let us never make a religion nor fanatic movement out of such principles, as our enemies do, let us not permeate this cause with a politico-economic color, but of a neo-humanistic color, which finds empathy to all beings through rationality. Through this rationality we may make our movement ecumenical, without it losing its primary essence, and penetrate subtly through those in reticence to change given their cultural programing. We may especially present to them ideologies, especially of religious, cultural and political kind, which assimilate to those they practice, but which includes these principles, so they may follow these principles regarding animal life indirectly, through our guidance and through our agents everywhere guiding towards more moral spheres.

Let us always make such principles possible through our knowledge of the human body, mind and spirit, and of the many sciences which comply with these principles, so we may have a plan B whenever they are led into possibilities of returning to the previous state of immorality. Let us, even so, allow for a margin for the disruption of these principles by the people to awaken, but let these be conducted with optimism as to improve and develop better and better over time and humanity become more spiritual and subtle. Always make an anteroom to follow these laws in some sense, and that its relativity may develop into absolute as we develop more technologies to provide alternatives, that, although artificial, may prove to be better for the environment and mother Earth and above all, to these creatures. Let us always minimize their suffering and improve the awareness of people regarding these principles as it may be within our reach. Let us provide them these alternatives through their own gastronomic culture, through agents which portray and pretend to act naturally so they may never truly awake to who really are the ones awakening them. Let us develop empathies in their minds even if they are nowhere to be found; through psychological and social engineering, let us develop morales in their beliefs through secret agents pertaining to be chiefs of their culture, and let us infiltrate and utilize religions or sub-religions akin to those practiced by them to persuade to take on these practices. Whenever our enemies execute any of such practices against these creatures, let us utilize all means by which we can stop them, let us, whenever any of such brutal and industrial murders of such creatures occurs without true reason, send positive vibration so they do not suffer much, let us protect through our spiritual abilities, and other of such kind on which we train such agents. Let us infiltrate and destroy the means by which such mass and industrialized murder may occur, especially when it is not done in a natural or rational way, but as the monetary and financial benefit of our enemies. Let us hack and infiltrate into such systems and destroy them from within, rendering fruitless their crude manifestations of ignorance and violence. Let us gather all means by which we can stop such events from occurring and by which we may raise awareness on the people of its malevolence and of its denotation as a drawback to our spiritual advancement. Let those in slumber receive abundantly of one and not of the other, so there disgusting desire of feeling their gule in such bloody terms, is directed against themselves, and so they may realize, and so those which see them from the outside, their animalistic and primitive nature, one by which they justify their own actions, and by which society will further develop in the right terms. Let the consummation of these principles be intimately related to the spiritual and neo-humanist, for this is a fundamental principle of human life, beyond the brutal zombification of society now occuring. So that one may benefit the other, building a ladder which leads to final consummation of these principles in such moral, spiritual and vibrational terms. Let people aware of how such immoral practices in such uncontrolled and irrational manner leads to a society of zombies, to war, hate, immorality, to satanism, and many other these events, emotions, beliefs, and isms, which will conduce to nothing but the self-destruction of humanity. Let us help animals in such ways so that they may help accomplish our objectives of changing society towards awakening and comic divinity, let Nature equally give of what it receives to those who break her laws and her composition and composite upon this planet, ultimately leading us to victory and the establishment of the rule of truth and justice, by all these factors and ourselves, against the disruptors of *dharma*, especially those who do so with all intentionality and knowledge of their actions, and less and more opportunity to those who are ignorant and scared given their self-imposed limitations.

- "As a united force, we recognize the intricate connection between political and economic dynamics, acknowledging the profound impact of economic structures on society. Our collective vision emphasizes a departure from materialistic principles, advocating for the construction of a society firmly rooted in spiritual ideals. We aim to extend our movement beyond mere economic necessity, emphasizing experimentation with alternative economic models in testing camps."

- "As a united group, we envision ourselves as catalysts for societal evolution, with economic systems serving as instruments for higher spiritual and societal progress. Our approach involves continuous experimentation, analysis, and adaptation of economic systems to meet our evolving societal needs. We prioritize flexibility and adaptability in economic experimentation, always in harmony with the broader spiritual context."

- "We, the awakened ones, which are part, in this same sense, of the militia of Mother Earth, will equally have to effectuate such awakening. This awakening is first, a conscious one, regarding the inherent aberrant state of mind of humanity, which may be changed by knowledge, wisdom, spirit, and reason."

- "Let us especially instill, from a young age, a sense of care for Nature in the minds of children, so a generation can grow with such naturality within their consciousness. We will equally in this process, create trained agents which will establish movements, everywhere possible, where society can be guided towards the path of the natural, and for the care of the same."

- "We will train and possess experts in mineralogy, chemistry, physics and any other of such fields pertaining to the so-called non-living natural world, by which we may understand the deeper feeling of our Earthy Mother, and we create the greatest and most natural (therefore, perfect) of the technologies, which will manifest impossible to surpass by our enemies."

- "Let us equally be rational at all times even so, and we may find that we may have to break any of such principles given very specific situations, especially as Mother Earth so disrupts herself to remove her diseased humanity. Even in such instances, let us utilize in all possible means by which our abanico of possibilities may expand so that we may not have to regard these laws and practices in relation to morality."

- "Let us always raise the voice of such injustices, through these front-groups and movements, let us especially do it through progressive and subtle means, when the mentality of the person is found to be in reticence to such ideals, and let us make abrupt whenever we found fervor in such individual."

- "Let us help animals in such ways so that they may help accomplish our objectives of changing society towards awakening and comic divinity, let Nature equally give of what she receives to those who break her laws and her composition and composite upon this planet, ultimately leading us to victory and the establishment of the rule of truth and justice."

13. Land, its appropriation and use

Secure land morally in abandoned areas | Utilize spiritual powers for protection | Efficient and innovative construction methods | Infiltrate society through relationships with the wealthy | Foster community support for defense | Collaborate with front-groups for objectives and secrecy | Diversify strategies for challenges and autonomy.

As important as studying time is for the success of our society, studying the many facets of the spatial intricacies will be of much use in the future, and in concerning the means and space to execute the same, nothing is more important than developing a realization of where we shall go and to what extend this place shall be led in such or such a way. This place shall be a medium by which we can tranquilly realize all objects while enjoying all the benefits of having configured such edifice in the correct manner, or of choosing one by which modification we shall enjoy of the same efficient mechanisms at our disposal. Just like a tiger knows the jungle, and the lion knows the savannah to get what he needs to survive, so does our society need to know its habitation, in order to survive in the most favorable conditions and that we don't have run difficulties everyday. Let us perfect the art of space, so that there is no limitation in the way we communicate with the land and use of the same for the consummation of our objects. Let us measure our land in terms of our time and vice-versa. Let us compose each of the stages of such appropriation and its use in such tempos that the time and the space are one and the same, and so habitation may render propitious to every circumstance which may come to between us and our objects. First, we shall only acquire the land propitious to our survival as an entity, ones in which normally inhabit, and others in which we direct our efforts in case of emergency, for example, whenever we are expulsed out of this place, in some way or the other, we shall always have this reserve place of habitation. Let our habitation be gathered everywhere, and anywhere, so no one discovers where we may be or we may go following the destruction of the former. First, when it comes to the appropriation of land, all of them are to be moral, but not necessarily legal, for the legislation within such countries do not follow the logical laws of morality, but only those imposed by the irrational and oblivious bureaucracy of the government. Therefore, whenever it may be possible, and any land or everywhere, there is no one inhabiting such a place, we have the right to take that place if we have nowhere else to live and effectuate our practices. No one can deny us this possibility, no one, not even the government has such a right when they are the first to disrupt it. Therefore, we shall appropriate any of these places as long as they have been abandoned or no one has settled yet in them. Whenever there is such a possibility and whenever we are persecuted by the forces of evil or not. If the place is abandoned, we may remodel the same and renew it, by first destroying it, or we may make use of the forces of spiritual nature found within such a place. If they are evil forces, and need to bring them back to life, we shall effectuate our procedures to turn the place back to a positive vibration, if there are disembodied souls within the place, we shall equally utilize our people who are experts in these arts and take them back to light and to let them follow their cycles. In some rare instances, we may utilize this evil energy and let this place be a prison in which we may put our enemies to test, in a manner of self-defense, if they indeed attack us. We may equally let this energy stay for some time to receive information on the history of the place, or some other information by which we are led to one or other mission or by which we may further study the mechanism of such paranormal phenomena. Let us seek this place where no one else in society dares to go, and which are in such a detriment and putrefactive state, physically, spiritually or both, that we are the only ones which are capable of transmitting such negative energy into positive energy, hence, securing for ourselves a place to stay beyond the absurd legislations of the bureaucrats, we may in time, gain the trust of the people by helping them, especially, in such spiritual manners, by which we are gained their belief in us and they entrust to such missions, in such way we have the support of the people, and, if the government pushes their hand to such or such interference, we shall let the power and protest of the people fall upon them. Let us, too, support the people by infiltrating constructors and other such workers, so that we may further lead to relationships which may lead us towards a place to live. If there are instances of such inhabited places, we may have no other option but to infiltrate through third party agents in the properties of these so that we may utilize them for our means. We may especially seek those rich people who have many properties, let us infiltrate us in their lives by romance and, and some cases, sex, by which we may gain control of the properties these people may possess, or let us, infiltrate in their life through friends, and convince through them to provide such places of habitation for us, willingly and freely, without any cost. Otherwise, these only be consummated in rare instances, preferably leading us to gain the support of these rich people by lending us their properties willingly and directly by our request. Let us enchant with our ideology and become a part of us, so that we may form a bond by which such properties are freely lended or given to us, without any of the more previously referred to risky enterprises. Let us, as missionaries, possess the willingness to take such risks for the continuance of our mission, let us be able to inhabit all such dangerous places and engage in all such difficult situations. Let us through our means or by hiring people apt in such arts, reform such places physically and spiritually, so that we may inhabit them without any interference, and let us always persuade such or such people, which may serve us through their property, to provide us with it utilization and the instrumentalization of the same towards our means. Let us exchange our services for the gratuitous lending of such or such property, for some time or permanently, so that we may render their appropriation through our services, and we may conduct it without any further complication. Let us always form a pretext or justification, always a true one, by which we may acquire such abandoned places and by which we may help such abandoned people who possess such properties. Whenever this or that illogical legislation of the bureaucracies are imposed upon us, we shall resist them by the support of those who we have given our services and defended from such evil phenomena, so that they may be obliged to protect us against such malpractices of the government. Therefore, let, in the appropriation of such land or in the support of such marginalized people, the same be part of us and act for us almost solely themselves, so that they, and the people within such a place may equally support us in our appropiation. We may also direct our military or police forces of security for our protection against these injustices and illogical procedures, but let them always defend us without anyone knowing they are doing so. Let us have people who are experts in such arts inhabit with us, so they become our cooperatives to the point that they may help us in such situations. Let us further protect ourselves by invoking the laws of Nature which permit us to inhabit such places righteously, and let them know that Laws of Nature are above all they defend created by men. Let us further, with such moral justification, defend ourselves and our properties with all means. In such a way we find pretext by which we employ our ultimate and accordant military power, by dint of all such official, dharmic police men and those in the militia which may work for us. And which will be equipped with all they need to protect us. Let us, in such situation, utilize our spiritual powers to protect ourselves, and whenever the situation so requires it, let us utilize all knowledge on the forces of nature and the laws of the all, for our protection, a knowledge which is only know to us, and by which we are at all times supported by providence, and other of the forces of supra-nature and extradimensional kind referred to in other chapters, and let us further utilize such powers whenever we may be in court or in prison, and let us support each other in such circumstances in the most subtle and camouflage means, and by (this in a fair and justifiable manner) suborning those corrupt people in the state, after which, we may transmute them, as we always do, towards our side of light. Let us, whenever we have no other option, buy such used houses or abandoned houses within the framework of the law, but always by the minimum price, and if the attainment of the same is superior to its cost, or rather, if the aftermath or possession of the same is fair enough to bring further light towards such a place or towards such an object.

Let us, otherwise, instrumentalize such creation by appropriating land and creating these buildings new. Let us build all such edifices always in our way, and in an innovative manner, let us render all the stages by which such a building, given its type and ways it deems to be constructed, be built with the most resourceful manners and by utilizing the least time and effort possible. Let the land be appropriated by the Laws of Nature, and let us create such buildings in places where it was previously deemed unbearable to human existence, let us place sources of water and electricity, and food, with our latest technology, by which such construction may be rendered easier. Let us, at all stages of building, seek the cheapest and most efficient way, by rending people's knowledge of all these in our inner society or through our front-groups. Let us have, to further ease the process, front-groups and front-men which shall work for us in such types of companies and provide with the resources necessary to ease the processes and resources by which such construction is to take place. Let us use the cheapest material whenever it is so possible, let us use occult technology which may precipitate the buildings to be constructed through new pathways, and let our efforts be directed and divided so that only 20% of the same result in 80% of the results. Let us control also, or collaborate with those who want to be in charge of such buildings so that we further ease the process and we may use them as front-agents. Let us create groups, cooperatives or enterprises which ar masked as new and innovative ways to provide to the people through a democratic process, to which we really agree, but which shall in turn, and in benefitting the people, also benefit us, and provide for an easier way to construct what we deem to construct. Ultimately, let us use a wide variety of front-groups to control the real-estate through all kinds of pretexts and masked objects, so that we might take control of such lands through these third-party companies, at which we may effectuate, through collaboration with them or infiltration in the same, our objects and the means we need hold for the consummation of the same, in any of such places, *tempos* or persons. Now, let us see, of what kinds these places ought to be and to what effects we may utilize them.

Dharmic lodges: This is the place where we usually meet on certain dates to refresh our memory on the path of Dharma, and the means by which we may improve and further perfect our spiritual journey and means. These places ought to be especially secured and protected and to be kept secret and free from any recording instrument as much as possible, otherwise, the righteous secrets of our society may be revealed to our enemies.

Temples or spiritual centers: Place of worship for us, which may be used as energetic instruments and by which all people are to be cleaned of their impurities, let us build them anew, or let us used old churches and other buildings from other religions and transmutate, to their true undistorted original religion outside of any kind of dogmas, and so we may further achieve such means by attracting people who prefer of these figures. In these places we may further help people outwardly and publicly as we have previously stated, through charity or support with food, and rescue in times of need, which are to be connected to these.

Educational centers: schools, universities and other learning centers, which we may use as further revenue, may be used to train any of such young people to be our agents and to fulfill any of such prophecies, while we teach them the spiritual practices we profess. Let us from these places, further train the smartest of men, which may be led to effectuate dints of knowledge and the further awakening of the people. And, ultimately, to train all those which may need to accomplish our needs and develop the latest top-level technology.

Resource and cultural centers: Places where we may place knowledge, antiques and more for the observance of the people, usually called libraries or museum, or any other of such kind, so that they may more easily awaken, let us further use these centers for further discussion and to improve the intellect and locate such intellectual people which may serve us later or to create a new culture, movement, entity or ideology as we may deem it better for us.

Community Service Centers: Places such as hospitals, food and clothes providers, environmental and emergency assistance, homeless shelters, legal aid centers, and rehab centers and financial counseling or any such kind where help is rendered to the community. Let further utilize such places for our means, and to infiltrate within the lowest and most impoverished and marginalized in society. By helping the people the people may help us, and we may help them awake from that same instance.

Guerrilla centers: Bunkers, dojos, military, police and security centers serve for our protection for the possible ordeal or transmutation of evil whenever such evil and dogmatic influences are affected upon the innocent people or civilians or against ourselves. Let us in this, train martial artists, security men, and other of such kind from a young age and let us further utilize these places as a fortress or back-up, whenever we may be in need or whenever we may need to test our new technologies or material and spiritual missions which may need some secret-protected-wide place which is appropriate for such experimentation of spiritual and technological nature.

Any of these places may be further interpolated or unified in their parent kind of centers, so that we may further simplify the process whenever it is appropriate or whenever we may be in need to effectuate in such a way. Or they may be intentionally destroyed by ourselves to make this or such people believe this or that, or more specifically our enemies, and to transmute any of their evils against in such a manners, manners by which we renew the old and bring light a new to such and such place in such or such situation. In such a manner, we may render our objects easily.

- The pursuit of strategic habitation involves acquiring land through moral means, particularly in abandoned or unclaimed areas. This approach encompasses not only physical remodeling but also spiritual renewal, tapping into forces of nature and addressing negative energies that may linger.

- In the quest for suitable habitation, the philosophy revolves around appropriating land propitious for survival. This includes areas traditionally inhabited and reserve spaces for emergencies. Moral justifications are emphasized over legal considerations, challenging bureaucratic impositions.

- The strategy extends to infiltrating various spheres of society, from relationships with wealthy individuals to influencing constructors and other workers. Rich people with multiple properties become targets for infiltration, utilizing personal relationships or ideological enchantment to gain access.

- In the endeavor to secure habitation, risks are willingly undertaken as missionaries navigate dangerous and difficult situations. Spiritual and occult powers are employed to reform physically and spiritually detrimental places, rendering them suitable for habitation.

- Protection is multifaceted, involving collaboration with military or police forces, invocation of the Laws of Nature, and the discreet use of spiritual powers. In legal or judicial confrontations, support is garnered through subtle means, suborning corrupt individuals to align with their cause.

- When faced with limited options, acquiring used or abandoned houses within legal frameworks is considered, always at the minimum cost. Alternatively, new creations are instrumentalized, employing innovative building methods and occult technology for efficient and resourceful construction.

- Front-groups and front-men play a crucial role in easing construction processes, controlling real estate, and maintaining a democratic facade. Diversification of strategies is emphasized to navigate challenges and maintain autonomy, ensuring the accomplishment of objectives.

- In summary, the strategic habitation philosophy encompasses a holistic approach, blending moral considerations, spiritual and occult practices, and strategic infiltrations to secure suitable living spaces for the mission's continuity.

14. On technology and artificiality

Artificiality births from man's mind, defying dharmic nature, inducing slumber | Enemies wield tech for control, enslaving under pretense | Danger looms as tech mimics humanity, leading to zombification, stripping dignity | Luciferian goals aim for a zombie empire, transifying humanity into soulless beings | Transmutation, the antidote: empower minds, enlighten collective | Harmonize artificial with nature, defend nature, empower humanity | Forge empire rooted in moral, spiritual, natural unity | Technology's essence: enhance human life, align with universal directives | Defend against enemies, destroy mediums, awaken spirits | Build the Dharma empire, embrace enlightenment. | Moderate artificiality, make it nature's extension. Follow universal order: spiritual, moral, natural. Tech as defender, not weapon | Minimize Earth's destruction | Integrate intellect, benevolence, principles for universal wisdom | Wisely choose fields, transmute enemy inventions | Transform the world, thwart adversaries, embrace enlightenment.

Artificiality is all that which has not been created by nature, but by the mind of man, while technology, is simply the material manifestation of the same given the subjugation of nature by man. Artificiality is now commonly aberrant creativity, aberrant meaning that it is against the dharmic purpose of man, it is against his inherent nature and role in the All. Such artificiality is one of the results of the current slumber in which humanity is embedded, and at the same time, it is the source of means by which such slumber is to be maintained. We see how our enemies utilize technology, not for the upbringing of humanity, but for its enslavement and privation of natural rights while they pretend to do the former. It has been created as to create such dependency upon such artificiality, that it ends up subjecting humanity to that of the creators of the same, or to this same technology given that it may acquire enough free will and consciousness to do so. Here technology begets a danger by which more and more power is trespassed to her, more and more abilities and tasks are given to her, supplanting humanity and, if such moment ever arrives, rebelling or upsetting the human contention over the rule of the world, intentionally or not, by own will, or by the will of our enemies. As technology become more and more human, humanity become more and more technological, and loses its face towards a state of zombification, in which dignity, honor and decency are not recognized given the compression of his mind in favor of the simplification of life, and not substitution of her tasks for a dangerous comfort zone, which is nothing but a vast nest for his own stupidity and aberrations. Humanity is therefore, "transifying", she is becoming transhuman, transexual, trans species, and any other "transfication" or aberration by which her intended nature is disrupted and her aspirations are those of a banal primitive nature, no matter how so-called technologically advanced they may seem. In such "transification" we see that humanity is nothing but being controlled by these luciferian leaders who enjoy the liberty given by the God they worship, and freedom to do as they please with no restraint, in total indulgence in the mundanity of materiality. We see here, therefore, that the true purpose of human life is not the improvement of her ingrained goals, is not even the easing of her deeds for if such was the case the world would not be so permeated by just the contrary in so many ways. The goals of artificial intelligence, as they has been established by our enemies are three in number:

1. *Turning humanity into soulless non-thinking zombies in a state of collective hypnosis by easing human life and the processes by which human life developed from youth to adulthood.*
2. *Given that human life has become more stupid, and her mental, spiritual, and even physical attitudes and aptitudes have been diminished, she may be more easily subjected, given that those processes in which were previously liberty are not submissive to the establisher of this same technology.*
3. *Given these two factors, one may allow more of the other, and these luciferians may more easily establish the empire of Lucifer, where we have a humanity of zombies,*

which are easily subjected to the will of our enemies and their many aberrant aspirations, and the many occurrences found theresince.

Thus, given this aphoristic simplification, of the subjects and objects of our enemy in relation to such technology, our equal simplification of the same are to be thought about by a process of transmutation of these into our positive side of the pendulum, saving humanity from such negative cycle, to our cycle of spiritual and dharmic order, such transmutation would be something like this:

1. *Empowering humanity into mindful, critically-thinking individuals in a state of collective enlightenment by enhancing human life and the processes through which human life developed from youth to adulthood.*

2. *Given that human life has become more intelligent, and his/her mental, spiritual, and even physical attitudes and aptitudes have been augmented, he/she may be more resilient, given that those processes in which were previously restricted are now liberated by the establisher of this same technology.*

3. *Given these two factors, one may reinforce more of the other, and these benevolent visionaries may more easily establish the empire of enlightenment, where we have a humanity of awakened beings, which are empowered to follow the will of our allies and their noble aspirations, and the many occurrences found therewith.*

In alas of deepening our methods on such matters, we may say that we will find moderation between the artificial and the natural, and that we will make the artificial so natural as to make it seem almost a part of nature itself, our technology, in its composition, shall follow the three directives of universal order which we follows, that spiritual principles, the moral and the natural. The moral is followed by building such technology with the sole purpose of enhancing and improving human life, with the sole purpose of driving humans towards their predisposed natural goal. Technology should not be utilized as a source of conflict or war, it should not be used to kill, nothing at all, but especially humans and animals. We should defend ourselves with technology but only with the purpose in mind of defending ourselves against the precipitation of evil derived from the perverse mind of our enemies against us or the people, or the attacks by which the same is accomplished, other than that the sole purpose is also of natural order. Our enemies utilize technology to destroy Mother Nature, and to disrupt against her laws. They build roads of a different color to the ground naturally found therein, the literally cement nature, they build edifices which are contrary to the natural patterns, totally in contradiction to the composition of such nature therein found, they create all kinds of machine by which fire is ignited to humanity or to the same extend to nature, they brutally subjugate nature and all her resources, while pretending in some other manner that they are doing the contrary. After all this has been effectuated, they utilize this same technology in their corporeal, mental and spiritual composition, they decompose the natural end of such means, and bring about their corrupt aspirations. We shall do exactly the opposite, and utilize this technology to find alternative ways to obtain such resources through newer and newer advancement in such fields, only extracting those resources when truly needed, and in a rationalized manner. In, creating such technology in alignment with nature, that it is unrecognizable to be technology to any first utilizer of the same; at the same time bringing about the least possible destruction to Mother Earth. Let us, after all these material aspects have been accomplished, or, in correlation with them, bring about the same mental natural principles, and accomplish this in a rationalized manner with the material aforementioned. Finally, when these two previous factors have been accomplished, enemies seek to bring about negative spiritual order, in which entities can feed on the zombified human beings, which in such a state of slumber, act as soulless containers to these entities, and their connection with these evil beings of transdimensional order can become more and more pronounced, until a unification with them and the enterprises of both of aberrant order are unified. Lucifer, the prince of the world takes a spiritual dominion over planet Earth! We know our enemies use all kind of such technology to mind-control humanity, to drive towards what they want in total degeneration and un consciousness, for this they have used electromagnetic transmitters, media, the internet, social media in which false idols, some of them created through artificial intelligence guide humanity, and many other of these secret pathways by which they secretly interfere with the positive spiritual aspirations of humanity, and bring more of their negative means and ends. Let us therefore, utilize technology for the purpose of destroying all their mediums of unfoldment, let us use weapons of spiritual order specifically designed for such purpose, and let use all secret kinds of technology to wake people up and improve and unfold their spiritual aspirations, which have been denied, in ignorance yet innocence by themselves, and in total intentionality and evil by our enemies. Let us finally, when all this has been decently accomplished, bring about an empire of Dharma from the Hand of God, and not of some ridiculous demonic extraterrestrial entity, but of the universal consciousness, of Creation. The only difference between them and us being that their technology seeks to bring chaos and division to humanity, while we seek to bring order and union. Union with ourselves, union with nature, and ultimately, union with God or Creation. Let us apply these principles of Creational order to all our technological enterprises, let us acquire the best knowledge, and the best seekers of such technological knowledge, the best technology, and the best inventors and engineers of such technology, the best methods to apply this technology,and the best appliers of technology, the best ideas of spiritual and progressive order for these technologies, and again, the generators of the same. There is no point at which such enterprises may go wrong having analyzed the information and having planned each point and technology according to such information in the right degree and manner. Having applied the principles outlined in the other chapters regarding knowledge {creates the foundation by which technology is created, we need it above all else, and we need to use this technology for the same transmission of knowledge in mass}, transmutation {we infiltrate in the technologies of our enemies and transmutate them into positive means and ends}, spirituality {we utilize the technology of our enemies for positive spiritual order and do the same with our technology, we create instruments to awaken people through invisibles vehicles of such order, without interfering with their will, or we establish the right environment for the same given are destruction of their enemies counterpart}, artifacts of ancient times {study history and the technology which they used, try to imitate it, personify their attitude and aptitude, and with the same create and fulfill prophecies}, our infiltration in politics, economies and military {infiltrate, transmutate and redirect such mediums of our enemies towards good, utilize instruments of war and security personnel, but solely for the war against our enemies themselves, and for our own protection from their various injustices, such as those prescribed in the political and economic order}, our contact with extraterrestrials {persuade them to present us their technology for good feats and solely for positive ends aligned with those of them, if evil, utilize these evil technologies to destroy the evil races through their own mediums or their human containers, which are our enemies on Earth}, our social structure, in the views of the insider and the outsider, {construct and utilize such technology in secret or in public, according to the degree to which our relation with the same is drawn and the effects brought on to society, decide if keeping construciton private for secret use, or secret construction for public use, let us decide if only displayed people or to our enemies, or any other of these contrasting factors } our close relation with Mother Earth {imitate mother Earth through such technology, being this an extension of her, and we our soldiers in the same manner, limit her destruction and annihilate the destruction effectuated by our enemies}, our apprehension of land and resources through covert means {utilize such lands and resources to build our technology and the degree of visibility we desire and let us find means by which experimentations and the buildings of these same edifices aligns to natural order}, our intellect {let us seek and hire the most intelligent of people or let us create from our own means and institutions, let us equally ourselves be the most knowleadlbe and intelligent, build pedagogic improvement for the creation of technology and the creative development of our alumni}, our benevolence as means to power {technology is used as means to power through benevolence, and this same power given in technological form shalll provide more benevolence of the same order}, our utilization of the universal principles {let us take deep engineering and utilization of the esoteric principles within the all, find the subliminal in nature, for the same in the creation of technology and the mechanisms this same technology relates to these universal principles}, and our use of emotions and values of such kind and wisdom {emotions, values and wisdom shall be key when creating technology, let us understand the creation and use of technology and the means by which these improve these factors and vice-versa, arriving at wisdom whenever we may commit a mistake}, shall nevertheless, all be used in conjunction and taken into account in regards to the creation and use of such technology, finally, we may choose to what area or fields of knowledge {medicine (telemedicine, medical imaging, genomics), environmental stuff (remote sensing, climate modeling), space things (robotics, satellites), computers (machine learning, cybersecurity), engineering (3D printing, nanotech), social sciences (big data, communication), agriculture (precision farming, biotech), education (e-learning, edtech), and psychology and physics (neuroimaging, virtual reality therapy, supercomputing, quantum computing) let us equally, transmutate any of those invented by our enemies for our own purposes} we may apply such principles and directives here before outlined, and we may in due time transmute the world from the plans of our enemies to our plans.

- Upon contemplating the nature of artificiality and its manifestation in technology, we discern a divergence from the harmonious order of the All. The luciferian misuse of technology by our adversaries to subjugate humanity prompts our introspection. Artificiality, born of aberrant creativity, becomes a tool for enslavement, contrary to its intended purpose of uplifting humanity.

- In this epoch of transification, humanity teeters on the brink of becoming mere appendages to the technology it creates. Our enemies seek to propel us into a state of collective hypnosis, rendering us soulless and malleable. The transgressions against the natural course of human development leave us vulnerable to their malevolent designs, orchestrated through the very technology meant to liberate us.

- To counter this perilous trajectory, we propose a transmutation—an empowerment of humanity into enlightened, critically-thinking beings. This metamorphosis hinges on the delicate balance between the artificial and the natural, guided by spiritual, moral, and natural principles. Our technology must serve the purpose of enhancing human life, defending against evil, and preserving the sanctity of Mother Nature.

- The moral imperative directs us to wield technology responsibly, refraining from its use as a tool of conflict or destruction. Unlike our adversaries, who exploit technology to subjugate nature, we aspire to align our technological advancements with the natural order. Our vision encompasses a world where technology seamlessly coexists with nature, minimizing harm and enhancing the well-being of the Earth.

- In the pursuit of this noble cause, we envisage the dismantling of the mind-control apparatus employed by our enemies. Spiritual weapons and covert technologies shall be employed to awaken the slumbering masses and thwart the nefarious influence of malevolent entities. The culmination of these efforts leads to the establishment of an empire of Dharma—a realm where order and union prevail over chaos and division.

- Our multifaceted approach encompasses the realms of knowledge, transmutation, spirituality, historical understanding, political influence, extraterrestrial engagement, ecological stewardship, intellectual progress, benevolence, universal principles, and emotional intelligence. As architects of this vision, we embark on a journey to transmute the adversarial plans into a harmonious and enlightened future. Through the orchestration of these elements, we envision a technological era where innovation becomes a force for positive change, safeguarding humanity against impending darkness.

15. On intellect, its means and ends

Intellect is power; it must surpass imposed limits for truth | Awakening transcends rules; intelligence expands beyond limitations | Devotion, not just intellect, is crucial for true life and awakening | Support those with will and spirituality; intellect is meaningless without the right attitude | Act contrary to enemies; transmute their forces for positive change | Build intelligence through will and spirituality; turn limitations into opportunities | Create awakened geniuses; direct intelligence toward truth, God, and spiritual awakening | Pair intelligence with will and spirituality for true awakening; go beyond scholastic skills | Question differences in intelligence; focus on building will and spirituality | Support unexpected sources; find will, spirituality, and awakening in unusual places | Develop intelligence from a young age with an emphasis on awakening, will, and spirit | Awakened geniuses bring innovative intelligence; maximize potential through efficient learning |

New ideologies emerge from awakened intelligence; change society toward a spiritual order.

The intellectual question is extremely important in the manner that it may convulse us to the greatest of bliss or to the greatest of calvaries, it may be equally, just as power, this being the one derived from the mind, as to create by which our enemies may further deceive people, or by which we may create bridges to unite them and help them. The intellectual question is not an absolute one in human societies, nor in the means by which we aim to change it. Intellect does not mean predisposition to truth, intellect simply is power of mental demarcation, just as physique is the power of the body. A person may be very intelligent, a person may know much, a person may deduce, induce, memorize and rationalize much, but these faculties of mind are worthless is they are not solely guided at the truth, instead they are being guided by dogmas of all kinds, which our enemies have masked as "science". But this intellect and this science is not of such order if it does not provide clear conclusions on truthful facts, and it is even more minute in comparison to truthful of this if it does not intend to ask or expand beyond the reality of the person. In such a manner, intellect is condensed and shrunk in such a way that it results in meaningless intellectual faculty. Intellectual capacity is only valuable if it questions all, and if it is derived from an open mind, which sees the truth beyond the incapacitated will of the wielders of the same. In plain language, it does not matter how smart a person may be, if this capacity does not, through will, expand beyond the limitations imposed by the wielder of the same. Intelligence by itself does not bring a person to an awakened state, if such was the case, millions upon millions of decently intelligent people on Earth would have already seen the truth, and the world would have not been in such a state of decay, then what is that they lack? They lack the capacity to see and discern beyond the imposed rules of scholastic skills. They only discern and rationalize this much, or that extent, but they are never, truly willing to GO BEYOND. To awaken is to BY WILL, GO BEYOND the COMMON RULE. If a person does not awaken this inner consciousness which questions everything and never accepts anything except after such examination, such person is incurring into intellectual mediocrity, no matter how much potential of the same he may possess, and he therefore, remains enabled to deception and the violation of his intellect by those who expand their minds beyond such boundaries, or by those which have created these same boundaries. He is therefore deceived, deeming that he WANTS TO BE DECEIVED, and he does not want to see the truth beyond this DECEPTION. He fails to see outside his circle of perception, he fails to rationalize in a different manner, which would better lead to the TRUTH, he fails to see the evidence, even if the evidence is placed in front of them in plain daylight. They have everything, they have eyes to see, they have ears to hear, and they have intelligence to understand, but they don't see, they don't listen and they don't understand. And above all, they have will, but they don't want to awaken to the truth. Thus, staying imprisoned by their own dogmas, as well planned by our enemies.

It is clear, given these previous points, that the solution to the issue of awakening people is not one of increasing the intelligence, but of directing the intelligence, no matter how minimal it may seem, towards awakening and truth; towards God. God does not seek intelligence from us, but only our will to direct such intelligence towards him, and hence towards the truth. If humans, even the intelligent ones, lack something, it is DEVOTION, and wherever and whenever there is no devotion, there is no expansion, there is no true life, and our power and capacities stay within the circles of conformity, mediocrity and deception. Therefore, we are to seek ways by which intelligence is not increased, for it is always there, but only to seek to increase the will of people to direct the same towards the truth. But this does not matter to us because what we seek is not intellect, but spirituality, a body and mind capable of saying the name of God and a person willing to express love to all, intellect therefore is secondary to us, given that we have it abundantly of Earth, and that it can be ever increased given certain factors. We have to find not intellectual people, we have to find people that, together with their intellect, have a capacity, borned, inherent or gained, to GO BEYOND THE MATRIX. Such people are surely very rare to find, one of the most common qualities of these people is that they are spiritual as much as they are intellectual, and that they hold a very profound relation with nature and Mother Earth, and many times, that this relationship extends beyond Earth towards other planets. Let us be experts at finding such weird elements of Nature, let us find people who have not merely intelligence, but will to expand this intelligence. Submissive intelligence is not worth a dime if it is not conjugated with rebelliousness and will for more. An intellectual zombie is still a zombie, an intellectual swallower of everything which is thrown upon their mouths, ears and mind, is still a submissive, inert being. He will still be submissive to our enemies, and hence they unconsciously become our enemies by such unconsciousness. Therefore, it is preferable for us to hire a common person who has WILL to see the TRUTH, AND GO BEYOND THE IMPOSITIONS OF THE MATRIX, than to hire genius who is subservient to our enemies in the minuteness of their capacity to properly expand and utilize their own potential. It is preferable for us to seek rebellious intellectual warriors who question everything, even if such intellect is not that strong, than to hire genius lamb for nothing, except for whatever is thrown upon their so-called intellect. Talent is nothing, if it is not paired with the right ATTITUDE, and the question of awakening is solely a question too profound to stay within the question of talent or intellect, but it goes beyond, it is A SPIRITUAL QUESTION. If we are to seek intelligence, we are to seek solely one which is paired with WILL and SPIRITUALITY, alike to the one expressed by ourselves. For the contrary to such, is precisely the attitude of our enemies. Our enemies are very intelligent, they have all the power, all the money, all the resources, and they control human population in such a state of slumber through the aforementioned, but they, have will, they have will to usurp will from the people, and they, have spirituality, spirituality to usurp intellectuality from the people. Hence, what ought we to do? We are to act precisely contrary to the manner by which our enemies act, and the forces they use are to be transmuted for our own objects, its positive counter of theirs. We are to use our intellect, our power, our money, and our resources, through their maximum potential and through the minimum and esoteric efforts and laws by which we may obtain them, so that we may seek everywhere in society, other than us, people who have to things, WILL AND SPIRITUALITY, will for the truth, and spirituality for God, true spirituality, and let us place them in our lines, hire or cooperate with them, in such a manner that the power and the influence we have acquired from our enemies through all the other mentioned means are passed to them, and society therefore, in as much as possible, and in conjunction with our other means, are given what our enemies much have, given that they have usurped the same from the people, and have given these faculties to demons which feed on the derivations in the personality of such people whenever they lack these qualities.

Other than this key element, let us refrain from questioning what is evident regarding the differences in intelligence among people, races, religions or any other condition by which intelligence may be limited, this is meaningless to us and this is what our enemies use and so much care for when believing themselves above the rest, and when they seek to divide people by such means, we shall only focus building intelligence by WILL AND SPIRITUALITY, no matter how initially low or minimum this intelligence may be, we shall always find ways to transmute (to find and develop other intelligence which may be more pronounced and the individual {there are many kinds of intelligence} and to utilize through other means and take advantage of such retarted people, not for evil, but for good, and for their benefit as we so do in other areas, let us support this so called illiterate or retarded people, and we may find support and power where no else has, we may find more will, spirituality and awakening in them than in any of the so-called geniuses {there have been famous non-intellgent saints}) and direct such poor intelligence at what really matters (the Laws of Creation; the Infinite power of our spirit), we shall only find ways to find the right attitude and the right spirit, and when these two are attained, limitations of all kind are destroyed. And that when such intelligence is attained we shall later use it, for more of the means by which it was initially rooted, namely; will, awakening and spirituality. We shall, in our schools, find all kinds of ways by which such intelligence may be ever-increased if it is so low as it said, we shall seek biological, psychic and spiritual means, intellectual tests and exercises of all kinds by which we may ever-increase such intelligence, we shall find find ways by which genes, mother and fathers may come to bring the most propitious conditions to bring an intellectually healthy baby to the world, and that such biological and genetic condition has been attained, it shall be further be increased with all means in our power, resulting in the greatest potential, which has no limits as to how far shall increased. But let his be secondary, let us rather pair this notion and practices to seek better and more intelligent people with a desire to awaken, let us create these geniuses from a young age, if we have no means by which we may find them in society, the best we could do is to develop such intelligence paired with awakening, will and spirit in our own schools and learning centers, rendering the production of such awakened true geniuses further easier. This awakened geniuses, will be keys in that they will allow us to develop and direct an intelligence which is innovative and out of this world, with newer and never before seen effective methods of learning, we will learn and maximize the potential of our intellect through a correct arrangement of the same and the stages which lead to such intellectual objects. Through this, we may deliver intelligence easily, we shall learn languages easily and shall our agents, mathematics, or any other thing shall be learned in such a precise and efficient manner; paired with naturality, that we shall provide ourselves with much expansion in our intellectual potential and learning capacity, so much more than our enemies, and we may find this intelligence to be paired with alternative rationality and discernment never before seen in society or in our enemies. We go hand in hand with our objects of awakening society and changing it towards a more spiritual order, this intelligence will provide our agents with more and more tools by which their areas of expertise or unfoldment will become a thousands times easier. We shall through this intellect create newer ideologies, bring about new knowledge and rationalization in all fields of sciences and arts; this, which are especially metaphysical and which encompass topics and discernments never before effectuated, will bring about new waves of scholastic and cathedratic paradigms, by which we may further bring about the new consciousness we want upon the sleeping people and ultimately upon Mother Earth.

- The intellectual question holds immense significance, capable of leading to either profound bliss or severe trials. It mirrors the power derived from the mind, a force that can be harnessed to either deceive or unite people. Intellect, akin to physical prowess, must align with truth rather than succumb to dogmas masked as science. True value lies in an open mind that questions everything and expands beyond imposed limits.

- Awakening demands the will to go beyond common rules. Intelligence alone doesn't ensure an awakened state; it requires a conscious effort to question, examine, and reject deception. Lack of this inner consciousness results in intellectual mediocrity, leaving individuals susceptible to manipulation by those who set boundaries.

- The solution to awakening isn't merely increasing intelligence but directing it towards truth and God. Devotion, not just intellect, is crucial. Seeking individuals with the will and spirituality to transcend societal norms becomes paramount. The focus shifts from intellect to spirituality, finding those with the capacity to go beyond the matrix.

- Acting contrary to enemies involves transmuting their forces positively. The emphasis is on utilizing intellect, power, money, and resources to identify individuals with will and spirituality. Supporting such individuals ensures that society receives what our enemies have taken—will and spirituality usurped for demons are to be reclaimed for the benefit of humanity.

- In addressing differences in intelligence, the approach is to build intelligence through will and spirituality, regardless of initial levels. Support extends to unexpected sources, finding will, spirituality, and awakening even in unconventional places. The goal is to develop intelligence from a young age, emphasizing awakening, will, and spirit in schools and learning centers.

- Awakened geniuses emerge as keys to innovative intelligence. Efforts focus on maximizing intellectual potential and learning capacity. This intelligence, paired with alternative rationality, becomes a powerful tool for agents in various fields. The ultimate objective is to bring about new waves of scholastic and cathedratic paradigms, fostering a new consciousness in society and Mother Earth.

16. Benevolence as the means of power; viceversa.

Power, rooted in benevolence for positive ends, is not inherently immoral | Power is an obligation in the laws of hierarchy and existence | Key is using power for moral, natural, and spiritual purposes, with self-control, knowledge, and wisdom | Power defends against abuse, aiming to defeat evil | Acquiring power through benevolence is legitimate, creating dependency for societal good | Helping those in power subdues and transforms, making power a manifestation of benevolence | Strategy: accomplish 80% of ends with 20% of means, creating a symbiotic relationship with society | Constant support ensures perpetual existence and appreciation | Spiritual practices extend help to God and Creation, securing divine assistance | Victory lies in a universal predisposition to help, manifesting for the sake of Creation and God until the end

Maybe the greatest problem within this world is that the positive side of the duality does not move as the dark side does, that this positive side does not utilize all the means by which it can beat its counterpart, and so the righteous gain the power to stand right and manifest upon Earth. We have already touched upon the transmutation of evil as means to acquire benevolence and manifest it on Earth, but it is equally important that such benevolence may be implemented with the object fighting evil. This surmount over evil necessarily requires power, for it is power that offers the means to strengthen this same benevolence. Power in such a scenario, when it is derived from benevolence, and utilized for the pro-creation of this same positive scenario, does not denote an evil path or an immoral intention or action. Rather, power acts solely as the means by which benevolence may be capable of destroying evil, and the means by which such power is to be ever incremented for the same cause. The acquirement of power, therefore, may just not be as immoral as it seems in crude or negative circumstances, if, on the contrary, such power is solely being used in a positive manner; to destroy evil, and bring about more of the same benevolence by which it was created, and if those who bring about such control or influence of the population control and rule themselves. For, in all certainly, no one has the legitimate right to rule others if that one does not rule itself, for in the same way there is deviation and entropy in their interior, they will so externalize. Hence, if we, as awakened people, are able to rule ourselves through self-control and other of such spiritual practices, and, if the sole means and ends of our power is that of benevolence, wouldn't it be better to sacrifice conformity and mediocrity, for courage and perfectibility? Isn't it much worse to contemplate evil and do not nothing, for the dogmatic intent of not acquiring power and escaping from the world and the problems like a coward? How does one stand above the other being that one only leads to more ignorance, evil, and does so in all its intentionality? It is irrational to think in such a cowardice and escapist manner, for it is not a possibility to escape power...

Power is as inherent to nature and existence as any of the other esoteric laws within the All, it is the law of hierarchy, and wherever and whenever there is a system, an order and clear arrangement of things, there must be hierarchy, one above the other, one guiding the other, and hence; power. Power will always be there, the question always is... for what ends is such power used, and to what extent does this positive end (if so originally intended) be revoked or corrupted by this same power? This same question, as it answers for each individual, is to be answered for the whole society, it is one of human nature and expression, which we classify in three: the moral, the natural, and the spiritual. These 3 are to be the sole utilization of power, the moral relating to the way in which humans treat their neighbors in the all, the natural relating to its place in the all (and his natural rights), and the spiritual relating to his union with the all, by dint of spiritual practices. These are the sole objects of power and human life, these in turn, lead to humans attaining knowledge, consciousness and wisdom. For cannot the latter exist without the former not the former without the latter. All these, which lead invariably to self-control, precede the extent to which power does not corrupt the person. If the person is crude, in deep slumber or ignorance, he will be ruled by power, but if the person possesses enough subtlety, awakeness and knowledge and wisdom, to gain the upper hand in such terms, he is assured to not be ruled by power, but to rule this with all rectitude and aptitude. In such situation, power is not an option, as explained, power simply is, always there as long as there is existence, and as there is always existence, there is always power, power therefore is an obligation, a necessity even greater than that of feeding our body or many other of such crude notion, for a society may exist without many of these, but surely it cannot exist without power, for the lack of power always leads to disorder if this is uncontrolled. Thus, we are obliged to utilize power, and to use it as self-defense against those who incur in its abuse and malutilization, in hopes that good may beat evil. But let us never fall prey to such or such temptations or egoistic and egocentric emotions and sensations, let us always know of the temporality and responsibility of holding such power, and that such power surely is simply the means for positive ends, and not the end of negative means. And in the same legitimate way, as power is to be used for good, in all its evidence and inherent necessity, we shall use it as the ends to be attained with benevolence. Because, just as evil; violence and any of these immoral acts, can be utilized to acquire power, so we can utilize goodness to bring about the same power. We can use our charity and universal neo-humanistic consideration and empathy with all, to gain the upper hand of all, but that this object may solely be the means by which more of the former to be printed in the social arenas. It is legitimate to desire power, if the means and ends of this power are legitimate. Hence, it is not immoral of our part to desire and acquire part through benevolence, for in no way can we escape, and in no way can we choose anything other than evil or this same positive counterpart now aforementioned. Therefore, let us be good to all, let us render and provide charity and support in all arenas to anyone that may need it, let us construct hospitals where we may help the seek, let us give money to those who are in bankruptcy, let us provide rehabilitation to those who are addicted. Let us provide help in short, to everyone who may need it, and let the matching of such support be rendered to society, in the manner in which our hierarchy is ordered. Meaning, let our lower agents provide help to the lower masses in society, and let our upper agents, less in number, provide support to those in power and help them, so through such benevolence, provided to the most malevolent, we may be given more of the same, and society may change. When these people, especially those in power, are receiving our support, in that same instance, are being rendered dependent to us, and hence, subdued to our orders and will. When such power is acquired in the cupula of society, we may use this same power to provide help more easily to all, (and in turn, gain even more power for this same good, and henceforth) instead of expanding much power for the lower means. In this way we accomplish 80% of the ends through 20% of the means. Let us therefore, help those in power as provided and explained in the modus in the other chapters, let us be all they have left when they have lost all hope in their delusion of evil, so that we may transmute this evil with our benevolence; and so they have no option but to provide us their power given the subsequent dependency upon our solutions. Through such manners, power is not handled to be the manifestation of evil and false pretended good, as our luciferian dualists enemies do, but solely of benevolence to acquire more and more power, and hence legitimizing our power, and making right and moral for us to be immoral, when the ends are more moral than the means itself, and when the attack is more immoral than the defense, and when this same end never to be corrupted but properly utilized. For this, let us be be like the the life energy of God itself, like the nurture provided by Nature, and all such element found within the same, which are completely necessary to life, and which human cannot live without, let human society, through our constant and genuine support and benevolence, be dependant upon our help as they are for the water the drink, so that our death shall means their death, so that our path to dry is their path to dry, and at the speed we disappear is the speed to which they cease to exist. In such a way, we are one with humanity, especially the good humanity, and these millions of combatants are so because of us, of we are the heroes that have helped them wake up, and hence by us they continue their path and soul purpose, and to us they shall render appreciation in the same degree. By providing help to all, there is no possible path by which we may die, or so does our movement and objects, for a new person will always manifest their appreciation for us by helping us whatever way they may be apt for and, especially those of especial power, aptitude and capacity, which will have to help, or they will come to at the same degree of us in their decease. We shall also, through our spiritual practices, provide help to God and Creation, and this God and Creation will offer us help, a help which is almighty, rendering us above those who only provide and seek help and benevolence from such minute in comparison demonic entities of various nature. Let us provide to all, and we shall receive from the same all benediction, let our provide help to only a part of this, and only from this part they may gain help, rendering us victorious by our universal and divine predisposition to help, which we will for Creation and God manifest, and for them we shall do so unto the end.

- In a world of dualities, the positive side struggles to keep pace with the dark. Transmuting evil into benevolence is crucial, requiring the use of power derived from benevolence to combat evil.

- Power, rooted in benevolence for positive ends, challenges the notion of immorality. It must align with moral, natural, and spiritual aspects, guided by self-control, knowledge, and wisdom. Society's existence depends on controlled power, preventing disorder.

- Awakening humanity emphasizes ruling with courage and perfectibility, rejecting the dogma of escaping problems. Desiring power through benevolence is legitimate, creating dependency for societal well-being.

- Constant support to those in power subdues and transforms, making power a manifestation of benevolence. The strategy aims to achieve significant ends with minimal means, fostering a symbiotic relationship with society.

- Providing benevolence, especially to those in power, influences society positively. Acquiring power at the apex allows for effective distribution for the common good.

- The goal is to establish benevolence as the driving force behind power, legitimizing its use for positive ends. The narrative draws parallels between benevolence and the life-sustaining elements of nature.

- By providing universal help, individuals become indispensable to society, ensuring perpetual existence and appreciation. Spiritual practices extend assistance to a higher purpose, securing divine intervention. Victory lies in a universal predisposition to help, manifesting for the sake of Creation and God until the end.

17. The esoteric laws, their factors and principles

Fixed laws permeate the All, indifferent, brutal in their mathematical essence | Utilize unchangeable laws; transmutation demands deep knowledge and spiritual practice | Everything is mental; thoughts create reality | Unite with God, harness the power of the mind | Patterns manifest in different dimensions; change internal patterns to alter external reality | Life is vibration; adjust to vibrations within the All, understand frequencies and energies | Acknowledge duality; strive for perfection in positive aspects | Transmute, infiltrate subtly | Cycles of change exist; identify and understand them for influencing outcomes | Every action has an equal opposite reaction; be aware to break negative cycles | Become universal alchemists, operate in the mental dualistic cycle, know multiform manifestations | Everything is psycho-causal; apply laws for ends and means, see beyond the apparent | Utilize, infiltrate, transmute for success and triumph | Master psychic and spiritual alchemy | Operate in contradictory yet practical manners | Flexibilize the application for subtle effectiveness | In the mental dualistic cycle, operate covertly for success | Become one with the All, reaching beyond tribulations.

There are fixed laws within the universe that permeate the very substance of All, the apparent, the relative, remains secondary when it comes to the ever-going application of such laws. These laws are not sentimental, they don't adhere to feelings or emotions, they are just in the most brutal sense of the word, they are mathematical, they are as it is. You cannot possibly change them, but you can utilize them in your favor in the apprehension of their knowledge. We may transmute them and direct towards our own means. This transmutation requires a deep knowledge on the peculiarities of universal expression and the Laws found therein. It requires spiritual practice in such a way and degree that it permits us to visualize the application of such laws, of learning their manifestation and the ways they may be received in relation to our means and ends. These laws rule the universe and the functioning of the supreme consciousness, hence they are the difference between the logical or the illogical, the natural or the unnatural, the perfect or the imperfect, and hence their comprehension and correct utilization are key towards the fulfillment of our objects and our success. We either take them into account and use them for our ends and by their invocation and representation in our enterprises we may relate the degree and way it is manifesting, the degree to which we are right or wrong, the degree to which we are a success or a failure. Henceforth, we shall take the following measures when it comes to such universal laws. The first set of laws we are to take into account are those expressed in the famous work called the Kybalion, in which the Laws of tantric nature, as promoted in ancient Greek and Egypt, were dispersed through such sages of these truths. The first of this law is the law of mentalism, relating to the fact that everything is mental, everything is consciousness. We are just a dream in the mind of the universal consciousness. We cannot possibly escape these laws of mentality, our thoughts create our reality, matter is solidified thought, and thought is subtle creative matter, of ethereal nature, and which everywhere gives life and consciousness. Everything may be modified through mentality, nothing is impossible for the universal mind. Hence we are to unite with the universal creator, God, and through such a way attain his qualities of omnipotent nature. We may equally, even without such a strong degree of spirituality, attain what we desire, what we wish, through the power of our minds, especially when they are used in conjunction and collective order. Let us equally utilize and transmutate this force as it manifest in ectoplasmic and crude elements, in short, in the material world, let us study the mental side and power behind everything, so that nothing escapes our perception and apprehension, so that nothing remain impossible through the infinite power of our spirit. Let us ask, and it shall be given to us, let us seek, and we shall find, let us knock the door and it shall open to us, let us believe and so it shall be. The law of correspondence refers to the manifestation of these same laws and patterns in different dimensions. As it is somewhere, it is everywhere, as it is above, it is below, as it is inside, it is outside. Let us change in such interior patterns and we shall change our reality, of external order. Let us change the infernal world, let us change the evil people, and we shall change the good people, let us study to the same degree, everything as it is manifested in all. Let us study all such sciences which are based on universal law, such as those of astrology numerology or others. Let us know the hidden subliminal patterns behind everything. Let us find correspondence, or similar patterns everywhere, let us find the invisible relatable intricacies within All, and above all, within ourselves. Let us see the A and the B, the B and the C, and their seemingly distinct nature will open a world of science and knowledge never before comprehended. Through such correspondence, we may covertly change point B, without anyone knowing that we do from its subterranean connection point A. So that the subliminal connection may construct us and transmute us to subliminal consequences of our objects, letting us through such ignorance of such keys comprehend and apprehend what we desire. The third principle is that of vibration, that of life, nothing ceases to vibrate, nothing is dead, but everything is life, nothing begins or ends, but everything vibrates and changes from one state to the other. We live, we vibrate, even after our death, our legacy, which is seemingly temporal, is rather eternal, for it always stays, given that it is spiritual in nature. Only that which relates to the all always stays in the same vibration, only the universal Creator does not change, and hence in the same we base our power. But even when it comes to the changing, we shall adjust to such vibrations, to such shaking within the very molecules, the very particles of the all. In such movement within the *corpus* of the All, we may the manners by which the vibrations, frequencies and energies of all are consummated, and the way by which we may change them in our favor. The 4th principle is that of polarity, of duality, this one is given, for the nature of all is apparently of such order. But we shall not neglect such duality to a second degree, we have very much explained our polarity in reference to knowledge and ignorance mainly, and also to good and evil, and all the others which may influence our goals. Our goals are not goals relative order, although they may so seem from the outside, our goals are only goals of good or bad, of knowledge or evil. We do not see grays except if it is within the relativity of human imperfection and the Laws of Creation. Otherwise, let us find all evil in good, and all good in evil, so that we may correct and clearly differentiate one from the other, and so we may finally come to be perfect in such a positive side of universal dualities. Let us in the same manner, find all irrationality in reason, and all reason in irrationality, let us find all knowledge in ignorance and all ignorance in knowledge, but let us not refrain from utilizing, infiltrating and transmutate the negative side, let us infiltrate in it as no else has done before, let our agents be like container of our will, but without neglecting their own, let them act and infiltrate in all negativity so that from within it may be destroyed, so that their attacks and may directed against them, as we have so explained in other chapter. And let us operate in such a manner with all, as universal alchemists. The principle of gender is just another principle within the principle of morality, it is just another bastion in the process of creation and destruction within the all. It is the true manner by which duality is entangled or diminished in infinite ups and downs. We cannot escape such principles found everywhere in nature, everywhere we see the nurturing and creative feminine, and the authoritative destroying masculinity. We shall not prefer one over the other, we shall justly apply what is to be applied in each moment, but not in brutal always in all cases, for we may apply such feminine energy through crude manners, or we may apply the masculine through subtle manners. The former may be the operation of nature, and the latter may be the operation of God. Therefore let us operate in such seemingly contradictory yet efficient and practical manners, as so does God, so that our attacks and application of such energy are unperceivable to our enemy. Let us equally utilize such knowledge and transmutation of the masculine and the feminine for the awakening of people, let us utilize such energy and handle it as a magician would handle water or fire, and let us flexibilize in our convenience. Let us do this with all other laws, and let us transmute them to change the consciousness of people from sleeping to awakening. In the law of rhythm we find that everything changes through time as the pendulum swings, through such changes, rything is created, and time is calculated, time does not exist but in the forces of translating and attraction of the planets in relation to their mother star. In the same way, our existence and the ups and downs of our life, its cycles, operate in relation to ups and downs, and therefore, in subsequent collective magnification, the cycles of society are the sum of all its mental factors in relation to their space within the all, these cycles or *yugas* manifested as an expression of such factors. Society is equally in constant change and civilizations come and go, with greater or lesser degree of spirituality and awakening. The current world is one of sleeping order, one of darkness, of ignorance and hate, but we have the tools, together with Mother Earth and our Celestial Father, to change such order in knowledge of the cycles of the All. We may dare to break, yet bring about those cycles in earlier manner given that we shall change the vibration of our minds, human consciousness cannot stand such swinging within the universal mind, when nature so wants something, when something is to pass, it will surely will come to pass, given that it corresponds to a previous action of the same degree. We shall identify such cycles within All, we shall identify them in our enemies, in their times of emotional dualism, rest and activity, masculinity and femininity, and when such given cycles is to be expressed, such given response is to be given in the same manner they aberrantly do the same to natural order. Let us find these cycles in the mind of the sleeping and our enemies more than they do, so that we have more knowledge of their destiny than them, and through we may secretly operate according to our means and ends. In consequence and conjunction with such laws, we find the supreme law, that of cause and effect, which says that every action, has an equal opposite reaction, and that every cause, has an effect of the manner and degree. As we sow, so shall we reap. Therefore, it is key for us to be very aware of the consequence of our actions, of the vibrations they leave upon their areas of influence, and the reaction which may be directed at us given such a process. The cause and effect are key to understanding the works of all, they are key to knowing what we do in this world, and what is the object of our life, and hence, they reason for the existence of our order, and the order by which this order consummates the order. Nothing can escape such law, society as it is now is given its carelessness towards such law, for everything we do unto others we do unto ourselves, and so humanity is in such a state of degradation, from one to the other, and what seems to be an endless cycle. We are to end such cycles of negative order, we are to transmute it to a positive one, we are to see the cause and effects others see only for their apparent self, for their ego, but we... we don't just see that apparent, we go beyond with our spiritual self, and that our soul and inner self is what truly holds importance, what does not change, the noumenal cause is the only cause worth attending. We equally see the substantial and spiritual cause intricate to all, we see the truth behind the state of everything and its origination point, which we certainly know is psycho-causal. Therefore, let us apply such laws in our ends and means in this summarized quote:

The laws of the All are expressed in an ever-going corresponding mental dualistic cycle of destruction and creation.

Let us operate in this same manner, and let us know all of its multiform manifestations, rendering our way into success and triumph over evil. Defiring the riddles and puzzles of the All, we may become one with the All, we reach beyond the mortifications of soul in this world, and we may reach our supreme goal.
Other laws which we may, in the same degree utilize, infiltrate and transmute for our means are these:

1.   The Law of Motivation
"Everything has a purpose for the creator and a function for creation, everything has a plan, everything is planned, no action is insignificant"
2.   The Law of Imagination
"The All is created by an Intuitive action of the Supreme Mind, everything is imagined, everything is fed by a mindless mind free of law"
3.   The Law of Feedback
"Every part is One with the Others, everything that goes comes back"
4.   The Law of Fascination
"Everything which is Alive is a product of mental fascination of the Supreme, these objects remain in balance by these waves of fascination in their patterns of commencement and termination"
5.   The Law of Intelligence
"Everything has an order, a balance, everything fulfills a logical pattern, independent of its apparent entropy"
6.   The Law of Necessity
"The polarities in the All remain at balance by the need of each others gender factors and expressions"
7.   The Law of Attraction
"Every polarity is attracted to and by the other as a product of fascination waves and gender difference"
8. The Law of Dominance
"Everything is part of a hierarchy, everything exercises dominion or is subjected, it varies in its manifestations and degrees there in"
9. The Law of Change

"Everything is in a constant state of change and transformations, nothing stays the same, in temporal, spatial and personal factors"
10. The Law of Cyclicity
"Everything expresses such Laws repeatedly through periods of time which differs in their intervals and degree"

Let us become, through these laws, universal alchemist, especially of psychic and spiritual order, let us see that which no one else seems to see, even more so now than before, and let us intricate their very expressions and transmutation our favor, as we may so deem it, or as our enemies may so ask for it.

- Law of Mentalism: The Power of Consciousness:

  The Kybalion, a revered text, unfolds laws inherited from ancient sages, starting with the Law of Mentalism. It emphasizes the dominance of the mental realm, asserting that everything is consciousness. Our thoughts, intricately linked to universal consciousness, shape our reality and hold transformative potential.

- Law of Correspondence: Patterns Across Dimensions:

  The Law of Correspondence unveils the interconnectedness of laws and patterns across different dimensions. By understanding and altering internal patterns, we can effect change in our external reality. This principle encourages the study of sciences grounded in universal law and the recognition of hidden patterns within ourselves and the cosmos.

- Law of Vibration: Life's Incessant Pulse:

  The principle of Vibration asserts the perpetual vibrancy of existence. Nothing is truly dead; everything pulsates with life. By attuning ourselves to these vibrations and comprehending their manifestation, we gain insight into the energies that permeate the universe and can harness them to our advantage.

- Law of Polarity: Embracing Duality:

  Duality is inherent in the nature of all things. The Law of Polarity prompts us to transcend the apparent dichotomy of good and evil, knowledge and ignorance.

Striving for perfection in the positive aspects of universal dualities, we navigate the delicate balance of feminine and masculine energies with strategic and subtle applications.

- Law of Rhythm: The Dance of Cycles:

  As a pendulum swings, the Law of Rhythm asserts that everything changes through time. Society's cycles, mirroring the collective mental factors within the cosmic framework, present opportunities for profound transformation. By identifying and understanding these cycles, we can clandestinely influence outcomes.

- Law of Cause and Effect: Navigating Consequences:

  The supreme Law of Cause and Effect underscores the significance of our actions. As we sow, so shall we reap. Awareness of the consequences of our deeds and the vibrations they leave upon the world is pivotal. Through this law, we break the cycle of negativity, transmuting it into positive change.

- Exploration of Additional Laws:

  Beyond these fundamental laws, we explore additional principles such as Motivation, Imagination, Feedback, Fascination, Intelligence, Necessity, Attraction, Dominance, Change, and Cyclicity. Each law contributes to our mastery as universal alchemists, empowering us to discern hidden truths and orchestrate transformative change.

18. Emotionality, values and wisdom

Emotions are tools to overcome limitations | Negative emotions fuel societal negativity, benefiting enemies | Fear is crucial for evil; eliminating it starves evil | Courage, the antidote to fear, transforms society | Teaching courage creates fearless individuals | Transmuting hate to love, despair to hope, betrayal to trust is transformative | Strategic terror infiltrates and transforms evil | Mother Earth responds with negative emotions, emphasizing natural values | Neo-humanist morals promote compassion, love, and unity | Spiritual values bring forth victory, externalizing wisdom | Success in the spiritual realm should be shared in the material, spreading wisdom | Redirecting negative emotions is crucial for understanding humanity's purpose | Transmuting negativity into positivity distinguishes wisdom from oblivion | Harnessing ignorance strategically transforms negativity | The goal is to transmute all negativity into positivity, utilizing wisdom | Through emotion transmutation, enemy destruction, and knowledge dissemination, we awaken and transform society.

Just as important as our beliefs and thoughts are our emotions. Emotions are very important, they are the manner by which we may react to the external world, the abilities by which we may overcome the limitations and difficulties drawn therein. These emotions and these values, in this era are purely within the negative side of the spectrum, we see that our enemies, and the entities they render worship to, benefit and feed on these emotions of negative kind. Every emotion and every value we hold as a principle in our life will manifest as a vibration, a frequency and energy, and from these emanations, held as collective mantras throughout the society, are a vast buffet for these entities, and for the more and more vibrations of the same kind, procreating a never-ending cycle of indulgence in such negative acts. If we look closely at the reasons by which people do no wake up, or seem to have no intention, conscious or unconscious, to realize the truth, is because they may be good people, and they may know, but they are afraid of being different, they are afraid of marginalization, they are afraid of our enemies stepping on them to keep in this same state. When fear gains the upper-hand, society and people, together with their innocence, become a victim of such strong sentiments, and they remain in profound reticence to go beyond what has been prescribed to them. Fear destroys their very souls, their very independence, a mental independence which provides true critical thinking, which is to evidently lead to the truth. In this battle between good and evil, fear is one of the keys, one of the most important foods by which evil manifests as the vacuum of good, fear is the link by which evil takes advantage of good. If benevolence ceases to fear, there is no food for evil, thus leading to the death of the same. Therefore, we ought, in ourselves and for the masses, to procure to eliminate all fear, to eliminate all terror, to eliminate all that which creates all these things in people in whatever ways they may be and throughout all of society. Whenever our enemies seek to cause terror, we shall think to apply courage for people and for ourselves, to destroy such evil with this valor, to by such courage, cause more fear in evil than they may want to cause in all. When we may stop fearing them, they will have no option to escape, they will have nowhere to go, but to surrender to good, for nowhere in such a space they may have a place to go and maintain this same evil by such alimentation and terrorization process. Fear and courage are tools, tools by which we may awaken and eliminate such processes of evil in human society. If fear is expectation to destruction of ourselves, we shall transmute this fear to expectation of destruction of the same which causes destruction, or of creating means by which such expectations change in those enemies. Therefore, let us inculcate in all other means and mediums herein displayed those transmutations by which we may transform into courage at all times, let children in our schools be inoculated with this sense of courage from a young age, let them have means and exercises by which their fear ceases, by which nothing scares, let us teach them, through all means possible, to face fear, and have fear to nothing, leading almost to a state of fearless, which conjugated with spiritual practices, shall lead to a state where our alumni do not even fear death, and henceforth we build agents which act through whatever means and surmount the insurmountable, without much care or worry for their own life. By such means, fearless in nature, our agents and ourselves will destroy evil presented all throughout society, and in the same manner, our enemies will have no place where they may escape. Let us too, build idols and public figures which are equally fearless, and serve as role models for the youth, placing such values of courage in a way which they are idolized by the people, therefore, by these two means, building future courageous generations. Let us through all mediums, all our processes and organizations, such as those of physical, intellectual and spiritual kind, bring about such emotions and values of courage, let such battle of knowledge against ignorance, and of good against evil, pay much attention and care to such factor of fear and courage, for it is fundamental in the awakening of people and in the consummation of the societal transformation we ought to bring about. Let us apply terror, so we may portray to act as our enemies to them and the people, so we may infiltrate and transmutate, but let such terror only be utilized for such means, when in such objects we construct the preceding means, now, when such terror is not applied for such transformation of the same, we are to solely apply it towards terror itself, so that they may finally get of the same of what the give, in a worse manner than they so do, so that it may be suggested to their subconscious by that same reciprocate trauma, that they shall change and alienate with what has been described by us. Let terror be solely the means to courage, and courage the means to terror, which are later to be transmuted back to courage. Let such application of terror and courage on people differ based on such circumstances, whatever they may be, and let it be applied in the right degree and manner, according to the same exhibited by themselves. Let the same transmutative processes be equally effectuated towards the others, emotions and values. Let hate be transmuted to love, for in this same manner we render charity and care for the people, and together with courage it is one of the keys by which we may increase our power and means. Let's equally, change joy, for sorrow, despair for hope, betrayal for trust, insecurity for confidence, boredom for excitement, disappointment for elation, rejection for acceptance, indifference for compassion, and surprise for expectation. Let us equally transmute and infiltrate the evil counterparts, by appearing to be those, and let us utilize these negative emotions on the innocent people, only in the moderate manner, and to teach them the truth. Let these emotions and transmutations of the same be directed at wisdom, and the 3 key values in human life; of naturality, morality and spirituality. In the context of naturality, let these emotions and values be brought about with the support of Mother Earth, who is tired of the constant state of aberration found within human society. Mother Earth may bring about negative emotions, especially those of terror and trauma, but this terror is solely an answer to the original terror brought about by humans and the same carelessness by which they abuse nature they will be abused by her, in cooperation with the All, and we will surely be paramount in the transmutation of such energies. In the moral context, these values of wisdom are those of compassion and love for all, having for this a neo-humanist perspective, which is more universalist and unifying than the current one of extreme specism, brutality and divisiveness. And finally, in the spiritual context, it expresses the minuteness and ephemeral nature of our lives, and what really holds importance, which is the spiritual eternal and not the material passing. Let especially, in this context, bring in relation the values of patience, initiative and effort, so that with this last in important position and the two previous we may bring into fruition our objects, not only in the spiritual but in the material. Let equally in this spiritual sense, the points of concentration, emotion and idealization be of utmost importance to our life. And let us equally, all that which we do to be successful in the spiritual, do in the material, so that our spiritual victory may be externalized to the people, who need to interiorize our externalized vibrations of truth. Let us, through such redirectioning of all negative emotions and values, arrive at wisdom and consciousness, for only through trauma (abrupt negative emotions) may humanity learn the truth on their purpose upon existence and the eternal laws of spirituality, naturality and morality, to finally detach for addiction (perverted positive emotion) and bring about and seek the truth, all, in all and for all, and thereafter, bringing forth, knowledge and good, in place of ignorance and evil, which we, in such profound mechanisms, shall equally transmutate and utilize for our convenience and hence that of Creation. As the difference between oblivion and wisdom is simply one of positive or negative emotions, let us pay much importance to the transmutation of negative emotions in relation to ignorance and oblivion, for these negative emotions are the root of this, and let us find ways by which oblivious or ignorance may utilized in our favor, and generally, in the favor of all, so that all negative may transformed into positive, and wisdom and practicality (to which we owe much of our practices and symbolism and to which much attention, as we did with knowledge we shall provide in relation to the awakening of the people and the destruction of our enemies) may be found in the most negative and seemingly evil of all things.

- The significance of emotions cannot be overstated; we firmly believe they play a pivotal role alongside our beliefs and thoughts in shaping our human experiences. We view emotions as potent tools to navigate the external world, overcome challenges, and exert influence on the vibrations and energies within our society. In our current era, we assert a dominance of negativity in emotions and values, creating a feeding ground for adversaries and entities aligned with malevolence.

- Fear stands out as a key factor inhibiting us from awakening to the truth. We recognize that even when we're aware of the truth, we may be deterred by the fear of being different or marginalized. We emphasize the detrimental impact of fear on both individuals and society, resulting in a suppression of critical thinking and independence.

- The battle between good and evil takes shape in terms of fear and courage. Fear is depicted as a source of nourishment for evil, and we argue for the necessity of eliminating fear to starve evil. Courage emerges as the antidote to fear, capable of disrupting the cycle of malevolence. We strongly advocate for instilling courage, particularly in the younger generation, as a transformative force against fear.

- Delving into the strategic application of terror and courage as tools for societal transformation, we suggest that fear should be transmuted into courage, with the ultimate goal of rendering evil powerless. We encourage the development of fearless agents and public figures as role models, fostering a culture of courage and idolization of such values.

- Furthermore, we explore the transmutation of negative emotions into positive ones, especially in the realms of naturality, morality, and spirituality. We underscore the importance of aligning spiritual practices with material actions and the need for concentration, emotion, and idealization in spiritual pursuits.

- We propose redirecting negative emotions towards wisdom and consciousness, highlighting the transformative power of trauma in our quest for truth. In conclusion, we assert the importance of transmuting negative emotions, detaching from addiction, and seeking the truth to bring forth knowledge and goodness. Our ultimate goal is to utilize negative elements for the betterment of Creation.

www.ingramcontent.com/pod-product-compliance
Lightning Source LLC
Chambersburg PA
CBHW080915260726
48661CB00009B/3671